Cornelia

Cornelia – daughter, wife and mother of famous men – won her own enduring place in Roman history. Her sons' political successors, orators, authors and even Roman emperors revered her as 'Mother of the Gracchi'. In a time of moral upheaval and cultural innovation, Cornelia's drive and education equipped her sons for the new age.

Why, asks Dixon, should the mother of revolutionaries have continued to be admired – for her prose style, her fertility, her philosophic calm in adversity, her vicarious ambition – by the same arch-conservatives who blamed her sons for the decline of the Republic?

Dixon reminds us that this iconic Roman mother venerated by later ages for igniting her sons' fatal political ambitions and for proclaiming that her children were her 'jewels', was once a woman, not only a myth. She endured the deaths of her own ambitions with the assassinations of her two famous sons ('the Gracchi') in their prime. Her daughter Sempronia, childless widow of a famous general, was the sole survivor of Cornelia's twelve children. Dixon argues that it was Sempronia, dutiful to the end, who kept the family myths alive.

This concise compact book plunges the reader into the turbulent Italy of the second century BCE, when Cornelia and her family were at the centre of the culture wars and political upheavals that followed military conquest. Essential reading for anyone interested in women's history, political myth-making or the politics of the Roman Republic.

Suzanne Dixon is an Australian classical scholar and feminist historian. She has published several books and numerous articles. She is now a freelance author and teaches English. She is an Honorary Reasearch Consultant to the Department of Classics and Ancient History at the University of Queensland and an Honorary Associate of the School of Philosophical and Historical Inquiry at the University of Sydney.

Women of the Ancient World
Series editors: Ronnie Ancona and Sarah B. Pomeroy

The books in this series offer compact and accessible introductions to the lives and historical times of women from the ancient world. Each book, written by a distinguished scholar in the field, introduces and explores the life of one woman or group of women from antiquity, from a biographical perspective.

The texts will be authoritative introductions by experts in the field. Each book will be of interest to students and scholars of antiquity as well as those with little or no prior knowledge of ancient history or literature, combining rigorous scholarship with reader-friendly prose. Each volume will contain a guide to further reading, a brief glossary, and timelines, maps, and images, as necessary.

Women of the Ancient World will provide an opportunity for specialists to present concise, authoritative accounts, uncovering and exploring important figures in need of historical study and advancing current scholarship on women of the past. Although there is a growing body of excellent scholarship on the lives and roles of women in the ancient world, much work remains. This series will be the first of its kind.

Cornelia, Mother of the Gracchi
Suzanne Dixon

Olympias, Mother of Alexander the Great
Elizabeth Carney

Julia Domna, Syrian Empress
Barbara Levick

Julia Augusti, The Emperor's Daughter
Elaine Fantham

Cornelia
Mother of the Gracchi

Suzanne Dixon

Routledge
Taylor & Francis Group

LONDON AND NEW YORK

First published 2007
by Routledge
2 Park Square, Milton Park, Abingdon, Oxon OX14 4RN

Simultaneously published in the USA and Canada
by Routledge
270 Madison Ave, New York, NY 10016

Routledge is an imprint of the Taylor & Francis Group, an informa business

© 2007 Suzanne Dixon

Typeset in Sabon by
Keystroke, 28 High Street, Tettenhall, Wolverhampton
Printed and bound in Great Britain by
Antony Rowe Ltd, Chippenham, Wiltshire

British Library Cataloguing in Publication Data
A catalogue record for this book is available from the British Library

Library of Congress Cataloging in Publication Data
Dixon, Suzanne.
  Cornelia, mother of the Gracchi / by Suzanne Dixon.
    p. cm. – (Women of antiquity)
  Includes bibliographical references and index.
  1. Cornelia, mother of the Gracchi. 2. Women–Rome–Biography.
3. Rome–History–Republic, 265–30 B.C. I. Title.
  DG254.5.D59 2007
  937′.05092–dc22
  [B]   2006033829

ISBN10: 0–415–33147–1 (hbk)
ISBN10: 0–415–33148–x (pbk)
ISBN10: 0–203–39243–4 (ebk)

ISBN13: 978–0–415–33147–0 (hbk)
ISBN13: 978–0–415–33148–7 (pbk)
ISBN13: 978–0–203–39243–0 (ebk)

Dedicated to all my students, past and present, and to my friend Mona, devoted political mother of Sebastian and John

Contents

Illustrations

Preface
Biography and legend

> I have often wondered why we like to read books about the lives of other people. Perhaps we are interested in what shapes people, or maybe we're just plain busybodies.[1]

Why should we reconstruct and read the lives of dead people? Any biographer from classical antiquity could have answered that question confidently: to inspire us with good examples and to caution us against the wronguns. Tacitus famously begins his biography of his father-in-law Agricola with the statement:

> Even our age, uninterested as it is in its own history, has maintained the venerable tradition of passing on the deeds and characters of famous men to demonstrate how many times some great and noble virtue has triumphed, overcoming the vice common to lesser and greater states alike: indifference to good, and envy.
>
> (Tac. *Agricola* 1.1)

Few serious modern biographers would venture to make such claims, unless they were naive or perverse. The moralizing or inspirational style is now seen (rightly, in most cases) as cheap and trivializing. The buzzwords of modern scholarship change ('voices', 'subjectivities', 'layers' or 'faces', according to the date of publication), but scholars generally agree that we cannot hope to reconstitute a full or accurate picture of any life, including our own.[2]

I was an unwilling conscript to the task of writing Cornelia's biography. My knowledge of Cornelia's life before I embarked on this project focused on specific aspects – her dowry, her role in educating her sons – and I had no desire to re-tread old ground. My protests to the editors about the dearth of hard information were echoed by the publishers' referees. And I had made a strong case in my book *Reading Roman Women* for the idea that individuals could not be retrieved from history, that even named, historic figures were little more than foci for subsequent fantasy, their lives and motives (their subjectivities, in a word) utterly lost to posterity. These objections apply doubly to the Roman 'personalities' of the second century BCE, trebly to women – and goodness knows how many times to this legendary super-mother, a *grande dame* whose name adorned rhetorical litanies of feminine perfection rattled off in every Roman schoolroom; a woman revered by subsequent ages as exemplary wife, mother, widow, *mater dolorosa* and prose stylist *extraordinaire*, her austere femininity celebrated in sculpture, painting and even stained glass well into the twentieth century.

In the end, against my own better judgement, I ungraciously agreed to produce a study of the *Cornelia tradition*, an anti-biography which began from the premise that biography was a non-concept. And yet . . . while my rational reservations about the enterprise of reconstructing a life, above all one for which we have no fixed, dateable beginning and end, are greater than ever, I must confess that I devour written biographies of all types and seldom miss the many brilliant, short documentaries that justify the existence of Australian television. The lives of our fellow humans are eternally fascinating narratives, even to us jaded souls who acknowledge that documentary or life-writing are also fictions. To an ancient historian it is almost reassuring to learn that modern authors, dealing with purportedly factual, non-literary sources, are little better off than we are. I was struck by the similarity of the problems faced by my friend and colleague, Carole Ferrier, in writing up the life of a twentieth-century Australian woman, also an author and political legend.[3]

Cornelia was certainly blessed and cursed with living in very interesting times and this opportunity to explore her life and its context in depth has had its rewards. Inevitably, I bring to the task a very different mindset from that of the admiring authors of classical antiquity (and later), who were impressed by her wealth and ancestry, who praised her calm in the face of adversity. I have not been inspired by Cornelia, but I have drawn some inspiration from the example of A.E. Astin's 1967 book about Cornelia's cousin, then son-in-law, Publius Cornelius Scipio Aemilianus. Astin lamented the limitations imposed by the sources on any study of this period (pp. 1–2). Acknowledging how difficult this made his attempt at building a coherent portrait of his subject as a political figure, he nonetheless concluded that the effort was worthwhile and his excellent book vindicates him.

Like her cousin, Cornelia has been commemorated by the recording of some of her notable 'sayings', especially her famous statement, 'My children are my jewels' (Val.Max. 4.4), so perhaps we can claim to have a dim echo of her voice, even if we do not have her published writings, which were admired in antiquity.[4] Many Roman authors bore testimony to Cornelia's special qualities, including her literary skill, and to incidents in her life and her response to them. I am thankful that we have so many sources to worry over but there is no point in pretending we can ever disinter Cornelia (that iconic Roman mummy) from the layers enfolding her and her legendary sons.

Carving up Cornelia into chapters

Biographies often begin with the birth and childhood of the subject and plod chronologically through the life course. Happily, this format (which almost necessitates the reader skipping forward to the interesting bits) is seldom possible with subjects from the ancient world since we do not usually have that kind of detail. In this book, the starting point of Cornelia's biography is an examination of stories marking her life stages and an introduction to ways in which we might approach the task of separating the fantastic from the probable. Chapter 1 ('Fact and fable: sorting out the sources') introduces the reader to the key events and sayings of Cornelia's life and to their historical context. It also introduces the basic cast of characters and the themes to which I return throughout the book – the construction of legends associated with Roman political families and the questions of why and how Cornelia herself attained enduring iconic status in Roman culture.

My opening chapter therefore outlines the kind of ancient sources used in reconstructing Cornelia's story but their extensive analysis is not confined to that chapter. The anecdotes discussed in Chapter 1 have been chosen for their contribution (or not) to our skeleton biography – and for their entertainment value. They illustrate the nature of our sources and the ways in which they might be assessed. The anecdotes also relate to key events in Cornelia's life: betrothal, marriage and motherhood. Other stories, which focus on her characterization as a prose writer, as a political spur to her sons, as their critic, supporter and, above all, as their dignified mourner, are more conveniently discussed under other headings.

The most exciting potential source is dealt with in the second chapter – letters allegedly written by Cornelia herself. Is it possible, as some have thought, that some of Cornelia's own writing has survived to the present day? Cicero (106–43 BCE), born when Cornelia was either recently dead or a very old woman, is an important source for many of the events which impinged on her life. He believed that he had read letters written by her. Prose fragments are still extant which purport to be from Cornelia to her son Gaius. They are discussed in detail in Chapter 2 ('People, politics, propaganda') because of their political content. Plutarch's biographies of Tiberius and Gaius Gracchus, written late first/early second century CE, are clearly key sources. Cornelia's second most famous saying (after the statement 'These are my jewels') was her reproach to her sons, that she was known as mother-in-law of Scipio [Aemilianus], not mother of the Gracchi. Plutarch (*TG* 8.7) is our source for this reproach and for the claim that 'the people erected a statue to her as "Mother of the Gracchi,"' (GG 4). These components of the Cornelia legend, together with her son Gaius' references to her in his speeches (attested by various sources), are touched on in the synoptic first chapter, but dealt with in greater detail in Chapter 2.

Cornelia's role in the propagation of Greek culture and the new Roman passion for rhetoric, philosophy and literature feature in Chapter 3, 'Culture wars', which also considers her educational role and her choice of teachers for her sons. Cornelia's appearance in lists of exemplary mothers is linked with her hands-on involvement in her sons' rhetorical training and with her excellent written and spoken Latin. But her iconic status as a great Roman mother had many sides to it. In some contexts, she is praised for her devotion to her children and her good prose, in others for showing admirable dignity in the face of bereavement. Elsewhere she is held up as the model of a good wife. These exemplary roles and the sources which display them are explored in Chapter 4, 'The icon'. It is convenient to divide up the sources and aspects of Cornelia's life in this way, as long as we recognize that each such division has overlaps and connections with others. Family, politics, culture and the interests of current and later authors intertwine.

Taking sides

Ideas and personalities, however illusory, can captivate the most rational authors for centuries. Cornelia herself and her famous sons, the Gracchi, clearly made strong impressions on their contemporaries. Even in death, Tiberius and Gaius Sempronius Gracchus polarized opinion, and image-makers on both sides were quick to idolize or demonize them. Annalists and biographers who wrote much later retain the traces of rabid partisanship. The partisanship continues (usually in more polite form) in modern scholarship, so much of the 'evidence' needs careful consideration . It is always difficult for a biographer to steer a course between the venom of enemies and the adulation of admirers.

I remain of the view that we cannot reconstruct historical characters in any meaningful way and therefore remain bemused by the strong feelings aroused in fellow scholars by phantoms of their own creation. It is not a boast, more a cause for regret, that I have not fallen prey to the biographer's trap of infatuation with the subject. Nor can I say, as Astin said (1967: vii) of Cornelia's peer Scipio Aemilianus, that 'enough can be discerned to establish something of the characteristics of Scipio as a man and as a political personality'. Cornelia remains enigmatic, a daunting, almost inhuman symbol of the virtues of an alien culture. I eventually became mildly interested in exploring her political role, her philosophical underpinning and the active part she played in the creation and maintenance of the Gracchan legend. But the only satisfaction I have found in this task has come from my attempt to rescue her daughter Sempronia from oblivion.

So here, with all its faults and disclaimers, is my version of the life and legends of Cornelia – based, as they say of those made-for-TV movies, on a true story. Readers will, as always, bring their own interests and interpretations to my efforts and draw their own conclusions. I have kept scholarly debates to a minimum and based my material wherever possible on the ancient sources, imperfect and fragmented as they are. I do not pretend to see into the soul of the cultivated teenage Cornelia, daughter of a famous father, who was betrothed to a man of her father's vintage; or of the young matron Cornelia's way of coming to terms with the deaths of nine of their children, then of her husband. I can sketch in the kind of life this wealthy widow led at her luxurious villa at Misenum on coastal Campania north of Naples, where she drew the shining intellectuals of her day to educate her three surviving 'jewels' (Val.Max. 4.4), the children in whom she instilled pride of family and love of the new learning. The violent deaths of her two sons in their prime, borne in public with proper aristocratic calm, must have been a terrible blow to this formidable woman, supported in her later years by her daughter, the childless widow Sempronia, sole survivor of Cornelia's twelve children. Both women were, I believe, political forces of their time. Both surely instilled pride of family and political ambition in the children of the murdered brothers.

One of the many things we do not know about Cornelia is precisely when she died – just that it was towards the end of the second century BCE. She survived her husband by about fifty years, her elder son by thirty years and her younger son by twenty. Sempronia remained, a distinguished widow in her fifties, guardian of the wealth and reputation of a daunting heritage, to ensure that the family legends survived and that Cornelia was known, as she had told her children she wished to be known, as 'mother of the Gracchi'.

Acknowledgements

I wish to express my particular appreciation of the helpful response of Amm. Domenico Carro, retiarius of romaeterna (*navigare necesse est*). With typical generosity, he not only gave permission for me to use his photograph of modern Misenum (Miseno, Figures 3.1 and 3.2) but offered to provide it free of charge in whatever format suited this publication.

Figure 5.1 is courtesy of the Virginia Museum of Fine Arts.

My husband, Rob Wills, provided invaluable help throughout.

Some useful dates

Mid-Republic

BCE

218–201	The Second Punic War
195	Censorship of Cato (the elder), repeal of the *Lex Oppia*
168	Conquest of Macedon, Battle of Pydna
155	Heads of Athenian philosophical schools on embassy to Rome
146	Sack of Corinth, destruction of Carthage
146–133	Erection of the porticus Metelli

Late Republic

133	Dated from the tribunate of Tiberius Sempronius Gracchus
129	Death of Scipio Aemilianus
123–122	Tribunates of Gaius Sempronius Gracchus
110	Conviction of Opimius which heralds the *popularis* revival
110–100	Erection of statue to Cornelia?
	Temporary alliance of *populares* Saturninus, Glaucia and Equitius with Marius
	Censorship of the two Metelli, Numidicus and Caprarius
101/100	Trial of Metellus Numidicus, Sempronia appears as witness
	Consul Marius abandons *populares* allies
	Populares leaders murdered, optimate resurgence
after 31	Erection of the porticus Octaviae on the site of the porticus Metelli
	Cornelia's statue incorporated in it, probably with a new inscription (seen by Pliny the elder some time before 79 CE)

Biodata

Note that the precise dates are often doubtful. I have discussed relevant questions in the text (esp. Chapter 1) but I have throughout used certain 'working' dates for convenience, e.g. 190 BCE as Cornelia's date of birth, 175 as the date of her marriage.

BCE

183?	death of Cornelia's father, Scipio Africanus 'the elder' (*maior*)
175?	marriage of Cornelia to Tiberius Sempronius Gracchus senior
163	birth of Tiberius (the son)
?165–155	birth of Sempronia
150–146	Sempronia's marriage to Scipio Aemilianus
154	death of Tiberius Sempronius Gracchus senior
152	birth of Gaius
102	death of Cornelia?

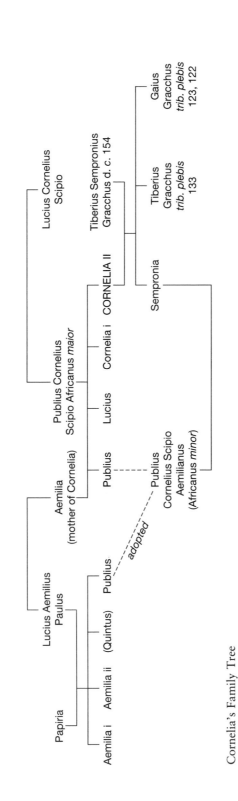

Cornelia's Family Tree

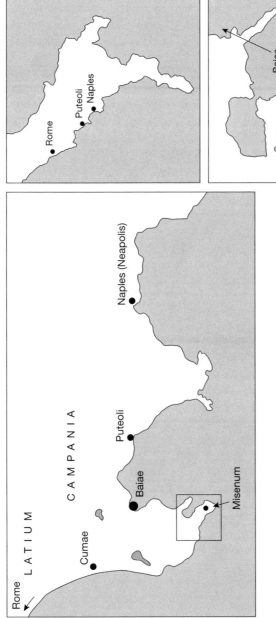

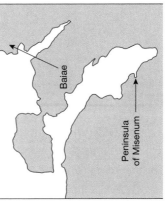

Map of Misenum

Reader helpline

Names

The general reader should take comfort from the fact that Roman names cause misery to the most hardened scholar. These tips should help:

> Sons and daughters took their names from their fathers. Women did not change their names after marriage.

> The name of a male Roman citizen had three parts, e.g. Publius Cornelius Scipio.

> The middle part is known as the clan or gentile name (*nomen*). Its female form constituted the sole name of a Roman woman – e.g. Cornelia. Thus two sisters would both be called Cornelia, while their brothers would be distinguished from each either by different first names (*praenomina*), e.g. as Publius Cornelius Scipio and Lucius Cornelius Scipio.

> Throughout this book, 'Cornelia' means the mother of the Gracchi. I refer to her older sister as 'the elder Cornelia'.

> Fathers and sons often bore identical names. I distinguish between the famous Tiberius Sempronius Gracchus and his father of the same name by referring to the father as Tiberius Sempronius Gracchus senior or, more simply, Tiberius senior.

> A distinguished general might add a *fourth* name derived from a spectacular victory. Cornelia's father became known as Publius Cornelius Scipio Africanus after his victory in north Africa (201 BCE) over the great Carthaginian Hannibal.

> But that's not all. Noble families sometimes adopted young men (frequently ones who were blood relatives) and that meant a change of name. On being adopted, a Roman man would take the name of his adoptive family, with the addition of a special form of his birth-name. Thus Publius Aemilius Paulus, adopted by Lucius Cornelius Scipio, became Publius Cornelius Scipio Aemilianus. To make things

even more complex, Aemilianus also took the name 'Africanus' after his destruction of Carthage 146 BCE, so he is often referred to by ancient and modern authors as Scipio Africanus the Younger, but throughout this book I call him Scipio Aemilianus or, more simply, Aemilianus.

'The Gracchi'

Because of their key role in Roman political history, Cornelia's sons (Tiberius and Gaius Sempronius Gracchus) are usually referred to in the plural as 'the Gracchi' and I follow this convention. In discussing them individually, I call them 'Tiberius (Gracchus)' or 'Gaius (Gracchus)'.

Do not forget the useful material at the end of the book!

- *Ancient authors*: these are listed, together with standard abbreviations and biographical dates (where known) in the annotated index of ancient authors.
- The general *index* is not only a guide to where people and topics can be found but includes brief explanations (e.g. of terms like 'optimate') and information about characters.

All translations from Latin or Greek are (of course) my own.
   Enjoy.

1 Fact and fable

Sorting out the sources

> Biographers are in the Frankenstein business: we make human beings. We put them together out of odd bits and pieces, not salvaged body parts now but scraps of information.[1]

Reconstructing a woman's life

'Facts' and dates

The sub-heading is ironic, for most of the 'facts' of Cornelia's life are contested. This book, though classed as a biography, is the story of a legend, of many legends. Cornelia, a privileged girl born into a famous Roman family early in the second century BCE, might have dropped, like so many nameless women, out of the historical record. Instead, her biographer is confronted with the need to sift and classify the many stories that surrounded her and mark the stages of her life. This can be confusing. In this chapter, I begin with an outline of what we *do* know (kind of) about Cornelia, then follow it with analysis of *how* we know and how sceptical we ought to be about the differing stories.

First, the basics: Cornelia was one of four children born some time between 195 and 190 BCE to the famous general Scipio Africanus the elder and his wife Aemilia. She married some time after her father's death *c*.183 BCE; she allegedly bore twelve children but only three – two sons and a daughter – lived beyond their childhood. Following the death of her husband Tiberius Sempronius Gracchus *c*.154 BCE, she devoted herself to her children's education, attracting the most innovative intellectuals to her maritime villa on coastal Campania.

In due course, her daughter Sempronia married, as did her elder son, Tiberius, who held the plebeian tribunate in 133 BCE but was killed before the year was out, without reaching his thirtieth birthday. Her remaining son was equally active politically and was also murdered after holding that office for the second time, in 121 BCE.[2] Cornelia was then in her sixties or seventies. She continued to live outside Rome, but did not withdraw from society. Far from it. Her personality and her famous hospitality drew the most cultivated people of the time to Misenum, where her villa became a social and cultural centre. Throughout her old age, she captivated her visitors with anecdotes about her famous father and sons.

Cornelia came from a very distinguished patrician family and married into a very distinguished plebeian family, both part of that small group of nobles which dominated the government and magistracies of Rome in the mid-Republican era.[3] She lived in a time of great change, following the defeat of the Carthaginian Hannibal and the expansion of Rome into the eastern Mediterranean. This is the period associated by the Romans with their own growing wealth, luxury and culture, features embodied in the long-lived Cornelia, who was a young girl (how young we cannot tell) when she married her much older husband. She lived to be a very old and distinguished widow, known not only for her male connections, but for her own wealth and culture. She actively promoted the new Hellenic style both prized and vilified by the Roman élite of the late second century BCE. Her children benefited from her promotion of rhetoric and philosophy. Her sons' skills in public speaking – typical of the new style – were famous, as was Cornelia's own style of written and conversational prose. So we know far more of her life and tastes than is usual in the case of such women.

She died a distinguished old woman towards the end of the second century BCE, at a date unknown to us, as is the precise date of her birth.

What we do not *know about Cornelia*

Let us backtrack a little. We are told that she had twelve children but the dates of their births are certain only in the case of 'the Gracchi' because we can count backwards from their tribunates. We do not know precisely when the nine children who died young were born or died. In fact, we lack information about many precise details which a modern biographer would regard as essential: the dates of her birth, her marriage and her death are all contested and debated by scholars. The ancient sources are agreed that she was a faithful wife and exemplary widow who would not contemplate remarriage (even to a king!) and she was held up for centuries as an example of a devoted mother. Moreover, she endured what was considered to be the most tragic blow of fate – the death of adult children, and those children among the most promising men of their generation – without self-pity or loss of control. Romans admired that kind of spirit. The praise is extravagant and almost uniform, the legends and romantic stories detailed. But, when you come down to it, we know few firm facts. Ancient historians are used to that. Many of us quite enjoy working out even the most basic dates from the meagre bits and pieces we do know, but the yield is pretty thin. Suffice it to say that, from the narrative perspective, Cornelia's life divides, like Gaul, into three:

- Her youth and her famously fertile years as a noble wife *c.*175–154 BCE
- Her widowhood from *c.*154, devoted to bringing up her three surviving children (154–135) and including the likely peak of her political activity 134–121 BCE
- Her glamorous but bereft old age and her withdrawal to Misenum from 132/121–102 (100?) BCE.

For the sake of convenience and readability, I shall henceforth treat certain dates as my working versions. Thus I shall opt for the compromise date of 190 BCE for Cornelia's birth and 175 (chosen largely for ease of calculation) for the date of her marriage, 154 BCE for the death of her husband Tiberius Sempronius Gracchus and 102 as the arbitrarily selected date of her death.

Sorting out the stories and the life stages

Whatever the precise dates of her birth and death, Cornelia lived a long life. Too long, for she outlived almost everybody she might have loved. But she has lived on longer still in the minds and tales of others. Some of the stories are confused and confusing, but we need to look at them to get some idea of Cornelia's standing in Roman eyes. They include *topoi*, or common-places, the kind of jokes and moralizing anecdotes which circulate in different periods, presented as true stories, and attached to different names, places and eras ('urban myths' in modern media-speak). Whatever we call them, they are highly dubious as evidence but, usually, great stories which are fun to hear and to pass on.

Cornelia stories generally illustrate something about her moral superiority or the regard in which she and her sons were held. They jump around the life stages which biographers would normally delineate. Perhaps we should treat them more as thematic events in the dramatized life of a Cornelia soap opera, as follows:

- the unmarried girl: a dramatic betrothal
- the proud mother: children vs. jewels
- the young wife: snakes and conjugal love
- the well-dowered heiress
- mother of many – but how many? And when? And of what sex? And . . .?

The unmarried girl: a dramatic betrothal

Cornelia's betrothal and marriage to Tiberius Sempronius Gracchus, a leading political figure and an enemy of her father Africanus, fell easily into the 'political reconciliation story' category. Romans could be savage and sentimental by turns and popular stories reflected this taste. Feuds and reconciliations were not just fictions but also genuine features of Roman political life, which could be melodramatic. Staged (and doubtless hammy) reconciliations in public settings, to the applause of onlookers, punctuated the vicious feuds, and were guaranteed crowd-pleasers.

Let me start with the most romantic and improbable (impossible) version of this particular reconciliation story. It is set on a holy day, when the senate gathered in force on the Capitoline hill for a grand feast to Jupiter. Tiberius Sempronius Gracchus (senior), sworn enemy of the Cornelii Scipiones (Cornelia's family), dramatically interposed his tribunician veto to prevent the great Publius Cornelius Scipio Africanus being led off to the very prison in which he had incarcerated so many of Rome's enemies. The senators all clamoured that Africanus seal this reconciliation with his erstwhile political opponent on the spot with the promise of his daughter in marriage. They insisted the two men embrace and conclude the arrangement before the dinner ended. Africanus acceded, yet another dramatic gesture was performed and the sentimental senators burst into applause.[4]

It gets better. For when the great general Africanus returned home after this eventful dinner, he informed his wife Aemilia that he had betrothed their daughter. She flew into the kind of rage women (or wives) are prone to (*muliebriter indignabunda*), protesting that she should have been consulted about *their* daughter's future. She climaxed her tirade with the clincher: 'I should have been included in the decision. Even if you were to promise her to Tiberius Gracchus!' Scipio happily replied that Tiberius Gracchus was indeed the bridegroom he had scored for their daughter. And domestic harmony was restored (Liv. 38.57.6). Well, it's a story. And it livens up lectures.

So what parts of this story could or could not be true? After all, Tiberius Gracchus was indeed an enemy of Publius Cornelius Scipio (Africanus) and was probably involved in the many attempts to hound him and his brother Lucius Cornelius Scipio.[5] And he did marry Cornelia. And it was normal to seal a new alignment or political deal with a marriage (Plut. *TG* 1.3). But the details of the anecdote do not fit what we know of Scipio Africanus' (Cornelia's father's) movements in the final years of his life, which he spent outside Rome.

The wealthy and successful Scipio Africanus, famous for vanquishing Hannibal in north Africa, came from a great family, the Cornelii Scipiones. In the viciously competitive world of Roman aristocratic politics, these apparent benefits conferred no immunity. At the peak of his fame, he was hounded by his enemies' accusations – a kind of Scipiogate. Scholars now are divided on whether there were ever any formal charges but Africanus took offence. Disgusted with the ingratitude of his fellow citizens, he retreated to his villa at Liternum in the mid- to late180s to pursue his cultural interests and died there within a year or two. He was therefore probably alive at the time of Tiberius Gracchus' tribunate in 187 or 184 BCE, but he is unlikely to have been in Rome attending an official banquet.

Cornelia's engagement is more plausibly dated to the period after her father's death, when his brother Lucius (Cornelia's uncle) was more vulnerable to attack. A political deal with Tiberius Sempronius Gracchus (senior) saved Lucius from disgrace and was sealed with his niece's betrothal to the new ally. We must relinquish the setting of the public dinner on the Capitol, the dramatic rescue from prison by the impetuous tribune and the betrothal by acclamation. Such embellishments typically accrue over time, as people forget (or ignore) the circumstances which would spoil a good yarn.[6]

Sadly, placing Cornelia's engagement to Tiberius Gracchus after Scipio Africanus' death *c.*183 BCE also requires us to discard the lively story of the domestic *contretemps* between Cornelia's parents (which is also told with other protagonists elsewhere).[7] It is less fun, but it makes much more sense to accept the alternative version, that the fatherless Cornelia's engagement was determined by her mother and other relatives in council.[8] The timing, after 183 BCE, accords better with the dates of Cornelia's known childbirths.[9] Livy passes on a series of conflicting accounts, only to throw up his hands – metaphorically, that is – and exclaim that there are just *so* many different stories (Liv. 38.57.8). Another good example to follow.

The proud mother: children vs. jewels

The best known story about Cornelia has her putting a Campanian woman in her place. The woman was being obnoxiously boastful about her jewels until Cornelia pointed to her children and stated, '*These* are my jewels'. It may sound arrogant and uncharitable to the modern ear, but the story served in the ancient world to illustrate her devotion to her children and her virtuous indifference to feminine fripperies and decadent badges of wealth. Comeuppance stories are eternally popular. This one is also told with minor variations of 'a Spartan woman' and of the wife of Phokion, but it is still associated above all with Cornelia.[10] And it could just have happened. She might even have been consciously quoting from or echoing existing versions of the story. Either way, it is now firmly embedded in her legend.

The young wife: snakes and conjugal love

It doesn't get any easier with the stories set in the marriage. The one which was repeated, even by sceptics, concerns the appearance of two snakes, one male and one female, in Cornelia's marital home. The pious Tiberius Sempronius Gracchus took them off to a religious official (*haruspex*) and was told that the snakes stood for the essence of his wife and himself – and, indeed, snakes are sometimes included in pictures of domestic shrines and associated with the *genius* of the male head of household (*paterfamilias*). He was told that if the female snake died first his wife would predecease him, but if the male died, he would predecease her. In view of his wife's youth, he chose to kill the male snake and, sure enough, Tiberius died not long afterwards.

Leaving aside any Freudian symbolism, there is nothing intrinsically improbable about snakes appearing in a household or about a pious ageing man seeking an interpretation from a state soothsayer. The fantastic conclusions drawn from Tiberius Gracchus' subsequent death are typical of the credulous in any age. We have good reason to accept this particular version, passed on by their son Gaius, as the kind of story which families sometimes treasure. Since this family was very political and occupied a special place in public discourse, it is not surprising that the tale would later be exploited by Tiberius Gracchus senior's sons for its faintly magical and heroic elements, to promote the family legend and to enhance their mother's personal prestige.

Cicero recounts the story in his work *On Divination* and cites Gaius Gracchus as its source. Presumably Gaius heard it from Cornelia.[11] Cicero uses the story as a device for challenging assumptions about supernatural events (*Div. I.36*).[12] Less critical versions of the tale are recounted by Valerius Maximus (4.6.1), Pliny the elder (*NH 7.122*), Plutarch (*TG 1.4–5*) and the late, anonymous 'author' (Auct. *de Viris Illustribus (57.4)*). Snake stories are sometimes associated in the ancient world with divine or semi-divine characters (heroes). This particular story insinuated itself into a public mythology, probably to elevate the importance of the family in general and of Cornelia in particular. It depicts her as a woman deemed by her distinguished husband worthy of his supreme sacrifice. And it emphasizes her prestige as daughter of Scipio Africanus, for snake stories about his birth and childhood also circulated during the second century BCE.[13]

The well-dowered heiress

Cornelia might have been loftily indifferent to the vulgar display of jewels but she was an extremely wealthy woman whose lavish lifestyle later became a byword. Her dowry, and also her sister's, were enormous. We have a reliable contemporary account from Polybius of its payment after the death of her mother Aemilia in 162 BCE. Modern scholarly interpretations of the incident he recounts may vary, but there is no reason to doubt Polybius' knowledge of the amount paid – fifty talents for each woman – from their mother's estate. Scipio Aemilianus' decision to pay both dowries as a one-off lump sum was the focus of Polybius' narrative, in which he cited it as an instance of his friend's generosity.[14]

The competing story, that the state supplied Cornelia's dowry, is easily disposed of. It is probably based on confusion between her father and another Roman general of the Scipio family.[15] In classical antiquity, the *topos* of the great general or statesman whose daughter was dowered at public expense had many variations. Sometimes such a story simply highlighted the gratitude of the state for the general's selfless public service. More commonly, the point of the story was the integrity of the general/statesman (who passed up opportunities for booty and bribes) or the degeneracy of his age, when even his splendid reputation was insufficient to attract a son-in-law.[16] The *topos* is quite inapplicable to the wealthy family of Cornelia and to her lavish dowry. Polybius' narrative emphasis is not on Cornelia's virtue but on that of Scipio Aemilianus. In both dowry stories, Cornelia is a bit-player.

Mother of many – but how many? And when? And of what sex? And . . .?

You would think some 'facts' about Cornelia would be incontrovertible. She was celebrated as the archetypal Roman mother, her virtue and fecundity exemplary. She was admired for the number of children she bore: twelve, according to Pliny the elder (*HN 7.57*) and Seneca the younger (*ad Helviam 16.6*), both writing two centuries after the event. Many scholars (myself included) have painstakingly examined the so-called evidence for the date of Cornelia's betrothal/marriage and the likely date of her husband's death (*c*.154), then tried to work out when she had those twelve children. Very little is certain. In fact, the calculations are so awkward that I have doubted the literal truth of those 'twelve births' and wondered if the number is an exaggeration, or if her admirers might have included stillbirths or mis-carriages in their total to bolster the later Cornelia myth of the iconic wife and mother.

The authors who insist on the number of births are not only late but often inaccurate about detail – Seneca the younger's main intention is to stress her undaunted spirit in the face of so many bereavements. He announces dramatically that Cornelia began with twelve children, and was reduced to two, namely her sons, as if he was unaware that Sempronia lived on. This oversight undermines his credibility. Pliny's prime interest was in Cornelia's freakish ability to alternate the sexes, which qualified her for entry into his encyclopedia of marvels.

The tradition that Gaius Gracchus was born after his father's death also has its difficulties and might be a later embroidery, to heighten the pathos of Cornelia's widowhood. Posthumous births would generally be mentioned by biographers and noted by the additional name 'Postumus' but no such usage is attested in Gaius' case by any ancient source, which would be odd in the case of such a famous subject.

What's left? Tradition and transmission

We can accept the general outline: widowed *c*.154 BCE, Cornelia did not remarry but devoted herself to rearing her three remaining children. She was celebrated for that devotion and for her refusal to remarry, although she allegedly received a proposal from 'King Ptolemy' (Plut. *TG 1.7*).[17]

Sorting out the differing source traditions for any topic is problematic. Cornelia's case is more complex than most. Any woman, however distinguished, is by definition tangential to the primary purpose of a Roman historian, which was to relate significant political (i.e. constitutional) and military events. Private life and political manoeuvres are also omitted or distorted by this focus and have to be drawn out of the main narrative or culled from the more eclectic *genre* of biography. The outlines of Cornelia's life therefore come through to us as they impinge on male lives and in those cases they are also mediated by the legends and images which surround such figures, particularly her father, the great Scipio Africanus, and her sons, the Gracchi, whose politics polarized opinion.

The myths and legends did not arise in a vacuum. In most cases they were conscious political constructions by the male principals or their supporters. Advertising campaigns lasted a lot longer in the ancient world than their modern equivalent: legends, like public buildings and memorable military feats, could continue to reap promotional benefits for a leading family over many generations. Elements of the legends would also be picked up and displayed by disinterested parties for reuse as amusing anecdotes or in inspirational lists. Valerius Maximus' books of quotes and stories conveniently arranged by theme ('On Poverty', 'On the Faithfulness of Wives') with moralising links are a classic example and provide some colourful if unreliable detail about Cornelia's life, as in the famous story about the bejewelled Campanian braggart being put in her place. Cornelius Nepos, a contemporary of Cicero, wrote biographies, histories of the Italian regions and probably a set of such *exempla*, of which little now remains, but that little throws light on some of the background issues of Cornelia.[18]

History can be quirky and a cunning man can take steps to ensure that Chance does not reduce his fame after his death. It has, for example, been observed that Tiberius Gracchus senior and Appius Claudius, towering figures in the second century BCE, have left far less imprint on the surviving sources than has Scipio Aemilianus.[19] Politicians in the ancient world were as quick as their modern equivalents to seize and to create promotional opportunities. Both Cato the elder and Scipio Aemilianus were forward-thinking. They illustrate the Roman process. They were not the only men to achieve high office and military success in this period but, thanks to their foresight, their reputations outlived them and both men were cited (and sometimes quoted) long after their deaths. While still a youth, Scipio Aemilianus enlisted the aid of the Greek author Polybius (c.200–118 BCE) in constructing his political legend.[20] Cato the elder did his own public relations. He had established a distinctive self-image as an aggressive orator and public moralist by the time Aemilianus was born c.185 BCE. Cato's published speeches and other writings guaranteed a long life for his characteristic sayings. Plutarch comments (*Cat.mai. 14.2*) on Cato's practice of boasting continually, in oratory and in print, about his own moral superiority.[21] By contrast, Aemilianus, who had confided his programme to Polybius, could stand back and modestly allow the historian Polybius to extol his many virtues and achievements for him.[22]

Cornelia's sons, 'the Gracchi', also had their legends. Cornelia's story combines elements of the Scipio Africanus mythology which arose early in the second century BCE and of the Gracchan legends which were consciously fostered by her younger son Gaius Gracchus. Cornelia and her surviving child, Sempronia, surely maintained the legends after his violent death, particularly in the final decade of the second century BCE.

The Gracchi had their enemies – to put it mildly. So, while Cornelia's own reputation was eventually immunized against any unfavourable association with their politics, the information we receive from authors like Appian and Plutarch is strongly affected by the opposed political traditions. Like Cicero, whose works provide us with important background and some specifics on Cornelia, Appian and Sallust were able to draw on a much greater stock of written sources from the second century BCE, including speeches and historical or biographical prose authors, as well as living history sources – those who had been young in the time of the Gracchi, or who were children, in-laws or close followers of participants in the events of the mid and late second century and had heard their stories.

Why Cornelia?

We return to the puzzle. We are left wondering why these stories have been passed on. It is extraordinary that Cornelia has any place in history. The records we do have pay little attention to women, even to those – such as Cornelia – who belonged to the most distinguished Roman families and influenced the politics and culture of their time.

And the second century BCE generally is not overly well served with surviving detailed, reliable historical sources. Most of the relevant books of Livy are lost to us and we often have to fall back on the Reader's Digest version of the epitomators. Not that Livy would be likely to tell us much about Cornelia – he passes on stories about her dowry and betrothal only because of their relevance to the politics of the 180s. His apology for recounting the *Lex Oppia* debate of 195 BCE and the female demonstrations which now intrigue us, reveals the outlook of a Roman annalist, who saw his primary role as chronicling the great events of state, interspersed with the omens and portents of each year: 'In the midst of great, almost unending warfare, an incident occured, trivial to relate, but which exploded in extraordinary conflict between opposed factions.'[23] In fact, the account which follows conveys the tensions rife in Roman society of the time about the pace and extent of change. The demonstrations and debates surrounding the repeal of wartime austerity measures served in the political forum (and in Livy's narrative) to dramatize these tensions. For once, women were not only signs invoked in political discourse but active participants. The idea of distinguished women taking to the streets and lobbying male voters directly might have shocked contemporaries but it has fascinated modern readers. Scholars are now very thankful that Livy saw fit to record this 'trivial' incident, but his disclaimer indicates a typical historian's attitude to the less 'dignified' aspects of Roman life.

Lobbying, informal canvassing, women's 'interference' in the political process – all detracted, in the view of traditionalists, from the glorious catalogues of military campaigns (ugh) and the lofty exercise of office by the great (men). We can readily see why Roman historians gave so little space to women. But that leaves us more puzzled than ever about Cornelia's insertion in the chronicle of second century BCE political life. Why does she fare so much better than other women of her time? Is it because she was the daughter, wife and mother of famous men? Well, perhaps. Her father, Publius Cornelius Scipio Africanus the elder, was famous above all as the general who ultimately vanquished Hannibal at Zama. Like Augustus after him, he achieved this victory with the help of a trusted friend, Laelius, who took charge of the fleet for the final north African campaign. Scipio Africanus (as I shall call him throughout this work[24]) was a larger-than-life figure and often highly controversial in his day, continually accused by political enemies of a range of flaws and even of crimes.[25] When denied an army in his consulship 205 BCE, he had raised one off his own bat. He was a prominent leader of the Hellenophile craze which seized Rome in the period after the Second Punic War finished in 201 BCE and a leader of the new, lavish style which went with it. He had immense prestige both at Rome and abroad and attracted (or devised) legends that assigned him hero (semi-divine) status, perhaps even during his lifetime. His fame does explain the proliferation of stories about the dowries and betrothals which cluster around Cornelia, who was distinguished even as a little girl by being 'daughter of Scipio Africanus'. But that alone does not explain the number and persistence of stories which attached to Cornelia herself during her lifetime and afterwards. Her elder sister, also called Cornelia, obviously had the same ancestry; she married a distinguished kinsman and produced a consular son, who was instrumental in the downfall and death of our Cornelia's son. Yet she barely surfaces in the tradition and certainly never had the iconic personal status of her younger sister, Cornelia.

(Our) Cornelia's sons, 'the Gracchi', born 163 and 153 BCE, took their name from their father Tiberius Sempronius Gracchus, who was himself a very distinguished man but who has since been eclipsed by his sons, although they did not live to achieve the high office he obtained. They became extremely famous. Or infamous. Viewed by some as champions of the people, they were generally vilified in the oligarchic historiographic tradition of Rome. Their tribunates in 133 and 123 BCE both ended in civil violence and in the death of the two men at a young age. The tribunate of Cornelia's elder son, Tiberius, in 133 BCE, marks the beginning of the turbulent late Republican period.[26]

But even the reputation of her sons is insufficient in itself to explain Cornelia's lasting renown. Other mothers of famous men are less well served. Leading *men* from the mid-Republican period (BC, or Before Cicero,

106–43 BCE) leave the barest biographic outlines on the sketchy canvas of Roman history. A modern commentator would put due weight on the alignments, marriage alliances and lobbying which characterized the highly competitive, concentrated politics of the incestuous nobility that ruled Rome, but we have seen that such topics were considered private and lightweight, not fit for inclusion in the grand picture of public life presented by someone like Livy.

A few women, it is true, are mentioned by name as *exempla* in the legendary, heroic versions of Roman history learned by successive generations of schoolboys – and, perhaps, as we shall see, some privately tutored school*girls*. The other famous Roman mother who comes to mind is Volumnia, who won her place in early Roman history at the expense of her son Coriolanus. The story has it that she and her daughter-in-law Veturia succeeded in turning him aside from his intended attack on his native city of Rome. Volumnia is one of a set of parents admired in Roman history for putting the good of the state before their natural favouritism towards their children (Plut. *Cor.* 33–6).

There is no such obvious explanation for Cornelia. Plutarch gives us a hint, in his lives of the Gracchi sons. He says that Gaius who as tribune of the *plebs* had proposed legislation targeting a man who had precipitated his brother's downfall and death, later withdrew his bill, giving as his reason that his mother Cornelia had intervened on the man's behalf:

> And the people were delighted and won over, for they honoured Cornelia as much for her children as for her father. Later, they set up a bronze statue of her and inscribed it 'Cornelia, mother of the Gracchi'.
>
> (Plut. *GG 4.4*)

Gaius' references to his mother in speeches were, like references to his dead brother in his speeches and written works, part of a conscious programme of political image-making which continued after his own death. The Gracchan legend was strong and surely kept alive particularly by Cornelia herself and by her daughter Sempronia, who was widowed in 129 BCE on the death of her husband Aemilianus. The statue of Cornelia was probably erected late in the century, during the period of a revival of the *populares*, a vague name for those who used the tribunician office to promote certain policies with a strong appeal to many voters who suffered in the economic upheavals of the period. Cornelia's statue seems to date to the same period as the forged or tweaked letter, purporting to be by Cornelia to Gaius and castigating him for his political recklessness. Plutarch's account (*GG 19*) of Cornelia's life at her villa on the Campanian coast reveals that, even in advanced old age, she persisted in her presentation of her sons as great heroes of history. Where did Plutarch get his picture of Cornelia's dignified old age? I suspect that his source derived ultimately from the testimony of Sempronia, who would have shared this villa life until her mother died. Sempronia, then a distinguished widow in her sixties, would have been the only one left at the end of the century with the ability and the motive to circulate stories about her family, so when at last the political wheel turned and others were eager to take up the legend and bask in the reflected glory of the Gracchi and their mother, the mythology was there, ready-made and maintained by the devoted women.[27]

Sempronia, guardian of the family legend?

Sempronia, one of the three children of Tiberius Gracchus senior and Cornelia to live to adulthood and the only one to survive into her mother's old age, is very much the forgotten woman in the Cornelii–Gracchi family story. Her treatment, far more typical than that accorded her mother, throws into relief the extraordinary richness of the source tradition on Cornelia. With few exceptions, modern authors generally follow the lead of the ancients.[28] We know from a story passed on by Valerius Maximus (3.8.6) that she served as the family representative who gave public testimony on the claim of a *popularis* tribune to be Tiberius Gracchus' illegitimate son, and so she was alive and active in 101/100 BCE. Her date of birth must, as always, be worked out from other circumstances. She might have been a little older or younger than Tiberius, if Pliny the elder was correct in his statement (*NH 7.57*) that Cornelia alternated the sexes in giving birth to twelve children.[29] Sempronia was older than Gaius, whose birth 153 BCE was around the time of their father's death. Sempronia married her famous kinsman Publius Cornelius Scipio Aemilianus, born *c.*183 BCE, who was a little younger than her mother Cornelia[30] (his cousin by birth, his aunt by adoption) but certainly much older than Sempronia herself. Plutarch (*TG 4.5*) states that Aemilianus was married to Tiberius' sister when the two men went to Carthage in 147 BCE, Aemilianus as commander, Tiberius as his subordinate. That indicates that the marriage probably took place some time before that date but we do not have a precise idea of the usual marriage age of noble girls in this period, so we can only assume she was between 13 and 16 (up to about 19) when she married. A birth date of 165–155 BCE would make her twenty or thirty years younger than her husband and a little older or younger than her brother Tiberius.

Sempronia is mentioned in two political contexts: the sudden death of her husband in 129 BCE and the trial mentioned above. Because Aemilianus' death without obvious cause occurred at a time of political upheaval (in which, as usual, he played a key role), rumours soon circulated about the possibility of murder or even suicide. Roman gossip often centred on the poisoning wife in such circumstances, but the idea that Sempronia, let alone her mother, might be implicated does not seem to have been a contemporary one. It is therefore notable that it took some time before anyone thought of implicating Aemilianus' wife Sempronia and his distinguished mother-in-law. Appian, writing *c.*80 BCE, includes the rumour among varying explanations for the death. While showing little serious interest in the suggestion that these women formed a mother–daughter political assassination team, Appian takes the opportunity to damn Sempronia in passing as not only childless but unlovely, unloving and unloved (*BC 1.20*).

Poor Sempronia. Appian has ensured that posterity should know she failed all the important standards by which women have traditionally been judged. The kindest classical scholars collapse this casual reference into Aemilianus having an 'unhappy marriage', others simply echo Appian or ignore her, in classic fashion. Did I hear the words '*plus ça change*' floating in the ether? I will now take the opportunity to insert Sempronia firmly into the historical record in quite a new light and one which is perfectly consistent with everything else we know. The historical record was maintained in this period with vigour, both by traditional methods within the ruling families and within the exciting new prose and rhetorical media which had taken the Roman elite by storm in the second century BCE. Gaius Gracchus is occasionally invoked by later authors as a source of information about family stories – the snakes in his parents' bedroom, for example – but Sempronia, who survived him by at least two decades, is an obvious source of information about the ageing Cornelia and her court at Misenum.

There are several parallels lurking in the crevices of the historical record which suggest that women often performed this function. They were even more prone to accept the task as a binding obligation, a purposeful mission if their family had dwindled and had suffered some disgrace or loss in the past. If we go forward in history, we find the daughter of the historian Cremutius Cordus, persecuted under the emperor Tiberius. His daughter Marcia kept his works secretly and maintained his memory, so that everything was ready once the opportunity finally presented itself for her father's rehabilitation.[31] The women of the Stoic opposition which suffered under the Julio-Claudian emperors and Domitian performed a similar role.[32] We know about those women and their role only because they happened to be acquaintances of men like Seneca the younger or the (also younger) Pliny, who recorded vital information in published works. Closer to Cornelia's day we have the example of Laelia, daughter of Scipio Aemilianus' great friend and political ally Laelius. Cicero praises Laelia's good Latin, stating that he had frequently heard her elegant speech. Laelia was an elderly lady when the very young Cicero was committed for two years to attendance on her husband, an expert in legal and religious matters. That Laelia (and possibly her sister, the other Laelia, who married the historian Fannius) was clearly an important source for the family stories on which Cicero drew, for example, in his work *de Amicitia*, set in 129 BCE immediately after Aemilianus' death, and for other works, such as his *de Senectute*, set even earlier in that century and featuring Laelius and Aemilianus as young men.

We hear nothing of Sempronia between 129 and 100 BCE, so we do not know where she lived out her long widowhood but it would be odd if she did not spend some of it in Campania (stronghold of the Sempronii Gracchi), with or near her ageing mother at Misenum.[33] Who would be a more likely source than Sempronia of stories about the lifestyle of Cornelia at this period of her life, her proud references to her distinguished sons in conversation? Who better to report on and respond to suggestions of her senility?

Let me go further. Who better to promote Cornelia's image and the revival of Gracchan political hopes than Sempronia at the end of the second century BCE, as the opportunity finally arose for reprisals and *optimate* forces seemed vulnerable to *popularis* attacks?[34] Who better to ensure piously that Cornelia should be celebrated as 'Mother of the Gracchi'? If her brothers had heard their mother's repeated complaint that she was better known as the mother-in-law of Scipio (Aemilianus) than as mother of the Gracchi, we can be sure her daughter – the wife, then widow of Aemilianus – heard the complaint even more often. And took it to heart.

2 People, politics, propaganda

Politics and pedigrees, 154–122 BCE

The personal was emphatically political within the ruling elite of the Roman Republic, a fact which the reader needs to keep in mind throughout this chapter, which includes a review of the personalities of Cornelia's family and of those supporters, connections and ill-wishers who affected their fates and their image in posterity. Cornelia was legally a member of the Cornelii Scipiones before her marriage admitted her to the Sempronii Gracchi, the family of her children. By adoption, marriage or entry into the Vestal priesthood, a Roman could change family membership at law but in human (and not-so-human) terms, their loyalties in each case were augmented, not simply transferred.[1] Marriages, technically the province of the all-powerful *paterfamilias*, were typically arranged by older-generation family members in accordance with family strategies – economic, social and political. The process was essentially as represented in the stories reviewed in the previous chapter about Cornelia's betrothal, but without the dramatic touches.

The Roman Republican aristocracy was intensely competitive. Its social institutions – including friendship, kinship, patronage, the law courts – were all implicated in this competition, which required each generation to renew and extend the family reputation, preferably at the expense of enemies. Prosecuting a powerful rival, opposing his candidacy for office or blocking his well-deserved triumph were standard reasons for consolidating existing alliances or courting new ones – by marriage, for example. Social debts would also be called in when a family member was standing for office, pressing for a lucrative and prestigious command or provincial appointment or fighting a prosecution from the enemy camp. Some of these alliances were fairly stable, extending from one generation to the next, but others could be very volatile indeed and breaches and re-formations were frequent. Cornelia's marriage represented one such re-formation, a reconciliation with an erstwhile family enemy (Tiberius Gracchus senior); relations with Scipio Aemilianus represent a breach.[2]

At birth, Cornelia inherited a number of intangibles valued by her fellow Romans more highly than the enormous wealth which was to characterize her. Through her mother Aemilia, Cornelia was the grand-daughter of a famous general, Lucius Aemilius Paulus, who had fallen fighting Hannibal. Her father, Publius Cornelius Scipio Africanus 'the elder', (*maior*, lit. 'greater'), was even more famous as the general who had finally succeeded in *defeating* the Carthaginian Hannibal and rescuing Rome from the rigours and anxieties of a long war on its doorstep. Things had looked very dark indeed when Cornelia's maternal grandfather fell at the battle of Cannae in 216 BCE.

But, as contemporary historians like Polybius were fond of pointing out, chance – *Tyche* – brings about sudden, extreme changes in human conditions. Barely pausing for breath after Hannibal was driven from the beleaguered Italian peninsula, the Romans seized super-power status, aggressively pushing into other parts of the Mediterranean and bringing back booty, slaves and Greek culture.[3] According to Roman tradition, this was the watershed and the old, simple style was gone forever (Polyb. 31.6–8). Never again would Roman generals be called from the plough, never again would Roman peasants be able to take for granted the continuation of their traditional style of subsistence farming. The Cornelii Scipiones were in the forefront of this economic and cultural explosion. The foundations of Cornelia's education must have been laid in this period of 'post-war' relaxation.[4] Her mother Aemilia, fathered by a man of legendary austerity and integrity, was to distinguish herself among other noblewomen for the lavishness of her religious trappings – almost certainly acquired as war plunder – and Cornelia herself would have been reared in a more luxurious style than any of her ancestors. The nexus between culture and luxury in this period is a strong one, a theme examined in Chapter 3 ('Culture wars').

We know that Cornelia was one of four children. Her older sister (also Cornelia) married a relative, Publius Cornelius Nasica. Her brother Publius Cornelius Scipio, whose poor health limited his political potential, adopted her cousin (on her mother's side) some time before 167 BCE.[5] This cousin was younger than Cornelia. The adoption altered his name (he was henceforth Publius Cornelius Scipio Aemilianus, to which the *agnomen* 'Africanus' was later added) and his legal status. He became a member of the Cornelii Scipiones and Cornelia's nephew. As such, he was responsible for distributing her mother's estate in 162 BCE, by which time Cornelia was married to the ex-consul Tiberius Sempronius Gracchus and had produced several of her children, including the younger Tiberius and probably her daughter Sempronia.

Aemilianus' gift to his biological mother Papiria (and, after her death a few years later, to his sisters) of Aemilia's famous religious equipage is the kind of thing that notoriously makes trouble within families. It would normally have been passed on to her own married daughters, the two Corneliae. Polybius predictably treats the action as an instance of Aemilianus' generosity but perhaps this largesse was approved by Cornelia and her sister, for Sempronia's subsequent marriage to Aemilianus suggests that relations between the cousins (= aunt and nephew) were good. Since her husband Gracchus died *c.*154, Cornelia must have played a key role in the decision to re-cement the existing family relationships in this conventional way, much as her mother had done in settling her own marriage at a family council (Plut. *TG 4.3*). When Aemilianus went to Carthage as a general (and consul for the second time) in 147 BCE, he took with him his fatherless cousin and brother-in-law, the young (15- or 16-year-old) Tiberius Gracchus, as he was later to take Gaius Gracchus (then 20) in his military retinue to Spain in 133 BCE. It was customary for noble youths to hone their military skills in this way, under the aegis of older relatives or family friends.[6] Relations between the cousins seem to have soured after an incident which occurred during Tiberius' quaestorship in Spain serving under the proconsul Hostilius Mancinus, who was besieging Numantia in 137/6 BCE. Scipio Aemilianus was partly responsible for the senate's repudiation of a treaty concluded by Mancinus, in which Tiberius had played a significant part (Plut. *TG 5–6*). The date of Tiberius' marriage to the daughter of Aemilianus' enemy Appius Claudius Pulcher is unknown, but it is likely that the marriage was concluded after this incident, and marks growing opposition between the two family members.

Aemilianus' motives for opposing the treaty were hardly disinterested. In 133 BCE, when Tiberius was in Rome attempting to promulgate his controversial legislation, Scipio Aemilianus was the commander in charge of the siege of Numantia and Tiberius' younger brother Gaius was serving under him. The precise setting and expression of Aemilianus' response to the news of the brutal killing of his young kinsman varies, but the purport is the same. The more popular one has him quoting: 'May any other who essays such acts perish thus' (*Od.*1.47).[7] So much for family feeling.

Scipio Aemilianus' quote would have lost nothing in the telling. It would not have endeared him to his wife, mother-in-law and surviving brother-in-law. Or to anyone else who was grieving. Even today, opinion continues to be divided on who was most in the wrong on that day when Tiberius and so many of his followers were killed. It must have been a *really* hot topic so soon after the horrors, when accusations were flying and both sides were claiming the moral high ground. It certainly confirms the judgement of Scipio Aemilianus' biographer Astin, that Aemilianus lacked tact and the more attractive political skills. Just as well he had a first-rate historian (Polybius) and satirist (Lucilius) on side.

On his return to Italy, Aemilianus wasted no time in flinging himself back into politics, going head-to-head with his remaining brother-in-law Gaius Gracchus and his old enemy Appius Claudius, both now members of the land commission which Tiberius had established. Clashes in 129 BCE with the 23-year-old Gaius over the judicial powers of the commissioners exposed Aemilianus to hostile public demonstrations. Then, suddenly, he died in his sleep (Appian *BC 1.19–20*). He was in his fifties. Suspicion later fell on the Gracchan camp and even on his wife Sempronia and mother-in-law

Cornelia, but at the time the death was treated as unfortunate but natural.[8] The triumviral land commission was probably hampered by the legislation Aemilianus had promoted before his death and its level of activity after 129 is debated. Notwithstanding, Gaius continued to be politically engaged and, like his brother, to make a great impression as a skilled and innovative public speaker. He was elected to the tribunate in 123 and again in 122. He instituted a more radical legislative programme than his brother and ultimately met the same fate, of political assassination, in 121 BCE.[9]

How political was Cornelia?

So once more Cornelia had to face that devastating loss, the violent death of a brilliant adult son. The sources agree that she bore this and all other losses with exemplary dignity, but they tell us little of her role in the politics that deprived her of her two dazzling jewels. Not that that should surprise us. Experts on the political alignments of this period all stress the difficulty of determining individual parties and beliefs from the scraps which come down to us – and they are speaking of ruling-class men who held prime constitutional offices![10] Cornelia's politics – both her activities and her likely beliefs – have to be deduced from even scrappier bits and pieces from diametrically opposed source traditions.

The Roman overlap between family and political allegiance makes sense of the actions of Cornelia in a society with firm conventions about public expressions of gender roles, but it poses severe interpretative problems for moderns trying to discern her 'politics'. I certainly do not subscribe to the Mitford view[11] that women's politics are always personal (nor to the implication that men's are not!) but that kind of attitude has always had a great impact on the way powerful women operated in public arenas and on the ways in which political women have been represented by contemporary media and by posterity.[12]

With these considerations in mind, let us review Cornelia's activities: both those we accept as true and even those which may be distorted or apocryphal. Her ambitions for her sons and her consciousness of her family's distinction are not in question and are generally seen by all sources as admirable. Her well-known insistence that she be known as 'mother of the Gracchi' (Plut. *TG* 8.7) is as likely to have been passed on to posterity by her daughter Sempronia as by those sons. The few source indications of specific events suggest that Cornelia was prepared to do whatever was required – including public actions appropriate to her sex and standing – to achieve her sons' aims (Dio *fr. 83.8*). She secured them the best possible education in oratory and philosophy and incidentally – or perhaps not so incidentally – exposed them to Stoicism and political philosophies which departed from traditional Roman elite concerns.[13] She would have ensured that her children received the appropriate assistance in fostering family glory: seeing to it that the elder son gained the proper training in leadership and military skills in his teens by accompanying Aemilianus to Carthage and arranging the marriage of her daughter to Aemilianus, reinforcing the connection with a key political figure of the age, one who was about to cement and expand his considerable standing by his destruction of Carthage in 146 BCE.

Then things changed. Tiberius Gracchus had invested his own skills and prestige in the treaty negotiated with Numantia. Its repudiation was a crushing humiliation for him.[14] Scipio Aemilianus' emphatic association with the senatorial decision marks his opposition to the interests of his younger relative (cf. Cic. *Brutus 103*, Vel.Pat. 2.2). While it can be dangerous to leap in and make too many assumptions about Roman political alliances, which are not always lasting or straightforward, the alignment by marriage of both Tiberius and his younger brother (by nine years) with Aemilianus' enemies in this period seems significant.

But their sister Sempronia was still married to Aemilianus. All things being equal, the commitment of Roman women to the interests of their fathers, brothers and sons was stronger than their loyalty to husbands.[15] Being fatherless and therefore legally independent (*sui iuris*) at the time of their marriages, Cornelia's sons were technically able to choose their own brides, but we can take it that Cornelia played a significant role in forming these important alliances.

Election to office required a certain corporate effort by kin and supporters of the candidate, no matter how distinguished. Scattered references throughout Roman history make it clear that even retiring women from lesser families played their part in soliciting support for their male relatives in these circumstances.[16] We can surely take it that the formidable widow Cornelia, unusually ambitious and in a position to be able to call on favours and dependants from her own side and that of her dead husband, would have lent herself in the appropriate way to her elder son's campaign. Once elected, he soon brought to bear his great oratorical skills in promoting the redistribution of public land to the landless citizenry in an effort to restore the traditional economic and moral equilibrium to Rome and to ensure the supply of proper peasant stock for the citizen army.[17]

Cornelia's training – both the example of her famously 'elegant' speech and writing and her provision for her children of the best rhetorical training of the age – found full fruition in her sons' oratory, which became so famous that, for ever after, even their detractors acknowledge their achievements, crediting them with special status in the historical development of this important new aristocratic skill at Rome. Nearly a century after Tiberius' historic tribunate of 133 BCE, Cicero cited him and his brother as examples of the fine balance between natural ability and training (Cic. *Brutus 103–4, 125, 210–211*).

And, as Plutarch's much more sympathetic account of the tribunate indicates, Tiberius was speaking to an audience ready to be moved. Even the fragmentary second- and third-hand accounts of his speeches on this subject – based on paraphrases and filtered through two changes of language (from the original Latin into Plutarch's Greek, then my English) – are stirring stuff and must have brought tears to the eyes of listeners:

> For Tiberius was a fierce and invincible champion of the poor, whenever he stood up on the rostrum, with the people crowding against it, and spoke for their benefit: 'The beasts of Italy have their special lair and their hideaway, every one of them has its fold or hole, while the men who fight and die for Italy have nothing but the air and light to call their own, but wander with their wives and children, without home or shelter. They're completely out of touch with reality, those generals who appeal to the soldiers on the battlefield, calling on them to defend their graves and shrines against the enemy. For not one out of so many Romans has a family tomb or ancestral altar. They fight – yes. They die. But for the luxury and wealth of someone else. They are called masters of the world, but they haven't so much as a clod of earth to their name.
>
> (Plut. *TG* 9)

This is not the place to debate with modern scepticism the literal truth of Tiberius' imagery.[18] The point is its undoubted impact on the men who flocked to the city to vote on his proposals to redistribute the common land (*ager publicus*), acquired by warfare and encroached on over the years by the wealthy, to the landless.

The Gracchan bills, since deemed revolutionary, were not entirely new. Aemilianus' friend Laelius had proposed comparable schemes in the 140s during his praetorship. Confronted with strong opposition, he had dropped them, thus earning the soubriquet of *sapiens* ('wise' – Plut. *TG 8.5*). So Tiberius and his supporters, powerful and prestigious fellow aristocrats, would have had no illusions that their programme would meet with universal favour. They would have planned their strategy well in advance of their election campaigns and scheduled the legislation for a year when they expected to hold key positions: Publius Mucius Scaevola as consul, his brother and fellow member of the pontifical college, Mucianus (adopted into the Licinii Crassi) as praetor, Appius Claudius as *princeps senatus* and Tiberius Gracchus, tribune of the *plebs*.[19]

The opposition – both to Tiberius' proposals and to those of Laelius a decade earlier – was not simply the knee-jerk response of wealthy Romans and Italian 'allies' who had long since subsumed Roman 'public' land and were outraged at the prospect of losing what they had come to treat as their personal property. At least as serious was the suspicion of rivals within the Roman aristocracy who understood the immense patronage benefits that would accrue to the three commissioners appointed to oversee the redistribution of public land: Tiberius and Gaius Sempronius Gracchus and Tiberius' father-in-law Appius Claudius Pulcher (Astin 1967: 92). The Roman oligarchy was based on mutual suspicion which led its leading lights to slap down any individual or family likely to rise too high above the ruling norm.

Let us pause and look behind some of the accusations flying about on both sides at the time and later: that Tiberius stacked the forum with his supporters and that his enemies were able to manoeuvre key meeting dates to times when his rural supporters could not afford to leave the countryside; that Tiberius' mother Cornelia appeared, dressed in mourning, with his young children at some public meeting to show their solidarity; that Tiberius and Gaius were systematically building up a huge basis of popular support in order to achieve an unconstitutional domination of the state – *regnum* in Latin, *tyrannis* in Greek, dictatorship in English; that, to this end, Tiberius and Gaius were attended by large gangs of armed supporters; that Cornelia organized such gangs from 'the countryside' to flock to Rome in support of Gaius; that she attempted to limit Gaius' vengeance (for his brother's murder) and revolutionary intent by her intervention and by letters begging him to stop before it was too late; that she conspired with her daughter to murder her son-in-law when he was undermining the commission established by her dead son and administered by her living son; that Gaius treasonably encouraged Latins to revolt against the Romans. And so on.

Well, it is highly unlikely that Aemilianus was murdered by anyone – suspicions voiced long after the event seem to be little more than low-grade gossip. The suggestion of a murderous conspiracy between Cornelia and Sempronia reflects generic Roman assumptions, such as the strong mother–daughter link, the loyalty of women to their brothers and sons and the tendency to attribute sudden, 'unexplained' deaths to poisoning and to cast the wife as the likely suspect.[20] In themselves, such rumours would not constitute serious evidence of political involvement.

Other hints in the record are firmer indicators that Cornelia was known for more than her good grammar and maternal devotion in her own day. Gaius himself gave her intervention as his reason for withdrawing the bill that would have kept the family enemy Octavius from public office (Plut. GG 4).[21] Plutarch, who passes on that story, states that 'the people' were grateful to her for this contribution to political harmony, that they valued her not only as the daughter of Scipio Africanus but also as mother of Tiberius Gracchus and that they 'later' erected a bronze statue to her with the inscription, 'Cornelia, mother of the Gracchi'.[22]

Like his older brother, Gaius was considered an outstanding orator, and his biting putdowns became famous. Plutarch refers with slight surprise and disapproval to the fact that in the course of such rhetorical give and take he sometimes used his mother's name in political speeches.[23] Ripostes to opponents such as: 'So are you slandering Cornelia, who bore Tiberius?' (Sen. *ad Helviam* 16.6) suggest that Cornelia was criticized in her own right, referred to by her son in a public, political context by name and linked with her dead and disgraced son. Both the criticism and Gaius' decision to counter it with her name and that of Tiberius are telling. Tiberius' memory and Cornelia's name carried weight, it would seem. Herrmann (1964: 88) and Barnard (1990: 389–390) both dismiss as rhetorical (i.e. 'topical') the suggestion that Cornelia had actually appeared with her grandchildren in mourning garb at some public meeting where Tiberius was speaking (Dio *frag. 82.8*), but give no reason for doubting it. It was commonplace – a *topos* – to mention the presence of relatives in courts because it was common practice. It was one of the few acceptable ways women could interact publicly with the political and judicial structures. What is interesting in this case is the suggestion that Tiberius' mother, rather than his wife, appeared with his children to work on the feelings of the assembled men.[24] This seems another indication of Cornelia's special role and status.

Cicero tells us that even Gaius' enemies were moved to hear him deliver his desperate, emotional appeal:

> Where shall I turn in my desperation? Where can I go? On to the Capitol? But it is awash with my brother's blood. Or home? What, and look upon my poor mother, desolate and beaten down?[25]

This final, evocative linking of bereaved mother and dead brother seems to have been part of Gaius' 'last day' lore and is imparted by Cicero as if he had heard of the incident from those present.

Gaius' rhetoric is not the only evidence for public criticism of his mother.[26] Plutarch records the accusation that she hired and sent to Rome rustic or pastoral thugs, presumably to protect Gaius (Plut. *GG 13.2*), and the dismissive suggestion that her dry-eyed references in her old age to her dead sons showed her senility.[27] Harmless old ladies would not have inspired such comments. Bauman (1992: 44) is quite right to see them as an earnest of Cornelia's political importance.

As to the accusations themselves, there is no question that Campania was an important patronage base for Cornelia and her children. Both Tiberius and Gaius had good reason to see and address its problems. They were well placed to muster voters from this region, which still suffered the consequences of having been a prime battleground of the Carthaginian and Roman armies during the second Punic War. The enemies of the Gracchi brothers and of Appius Claudius were surely correct, too, in their belief that these men had always intended to build a huge client base from the beneficiaries of their patronage via the agrarian commission and that Cornelia was at the very least privy to their plans in the years leading up to Tiberius' tribunate. It is plausible that the circumstances of Tiberius' death strengthened the resolve of Gaius, Sempronia and Cornelia to carry out the programme and to ensure that the family name be restored; that leading figures on both sides of the many political battles of the period 133–121 BCE were regularly attended in public by large crowds of supporters and that many of them would have been armed or chosen for their intimidating appearance. I see no reason to doubt that Cornelia herself came to Rome to lend the support of her presence as well as her name, where appropriate, to occasions furthering her sons' political ambitions. Even from Misenum, she would have been able to call on her wide-ranging connections, which extended well beyond the Italian peninsula.

Gaius was marked out early for distinction and the enemies of the family watched him carefully for signs that his ambitions – or the family ambitions – exceeded legal and conventional limits. He was 20 when he became a member of the land commission established by his brother Tiberius. He served on it for four years before its scope was limited by his brother-in-law Scipio Aemilianus. Still in his twenties, by the time he went to Sardinia in 126 BCE, once more in the relatively junior role of quaestor, he had cut a figure in the law courts and the politics of the capital and made clear his intention of taking up his brother's cause. In this relatively junior role, generally a stepping stone to a political career, he again made his mark. He managed to clothe the soldiers without cost to them (he was later to raise the issue of clothing the Roman army at state expense) and his family reputation and influence ensured that grain was delivered to Sardinia for the benefit of the troops. That denoted extraordinary patronage and influence.[28] It could also be related to his mother's continued connections with the many highly placed foreigners cultivated by both his father, Tiberius Gracchus senior, and his famous maternal grandfather, Scipio Africanus the elder. Gaius returned to Rome to stand for the tribunate and was criticized for leaving his post early, before his commander Orestes.

Plutarch's account of these years is sympathetic to Gaius and represents him as unjustly hounded by his – or family – enemies (*GG* 2–8). But Gaius, like his brother and other family members, was quick to draw on family connections wherever they were to be found. The inheritance of a few generations of conquest abroad, together with the acquisition of land within Italy, all consolidated by an ambitious mother who had taken up her residence near a major port, gave him vast stores of patronage and influence on which he could draw. His measures, like those of his brother, might or might not have been driven by humane considerations for the common man, but they would undoubtedly have extended even further the huge inherited family power base. And his family, shrouded in legend and semi-divine heroic cult tributes, had a recent history of unconstitutional achievement: his adoptive uncle and erstwhile commander and brother-in-law Scipio Aemilianus had, after all, managed to bypass the newly secured ladder of office.[29] His grandfather Scipio Africanus the elder had achieved his commands and first consulship in even more irregular circumstances and actually raised an army off his own bat. *Invidia* was readily aroused by much less than that.

Change is always disturbing. Conquest abroad brought wealth to the upper class but it fostered unrest in the lower ranks of the army and in the Italian countryside, source of manpower for armies that spent longer and longer abroad without ever gaining a proportionate share in the spoils. Rome was a republic which taught its noble youths the evils of kingship. The ruling families were in the habit of eyeing competitors with suspicion and slapping down individuals who stood out. It was not surprising that the family enemies did what they could to check Gaius, a man with an immense heritage of prestige and patronage and a just grievance centred on a brother whose name could still stir the voters; Gaius, who in his twenties demonstrated outstanding abilities and the desire and means to exploit them to the full. His fellow nobles were by now also schooled in Greek philosophy and history. They had heard of 'tyrants', aristocrats who built up huge popular support and established unconstitutional monarchies. In hindsight, we know that it took another century before that process was completed at Rome, but things might have looked different to the enemies of Cornelia's surviving son.

Cornelia, Sempronia and post-Gracchan propaganda (122–100 BCE)

Cornelia's long life was almost defined by death. Fortunately, death was not necessarily the end. Views differ on precisely when the famous villa at Misenum became Cornelia's primary residence. But whether it was from the time of her younger son's death in 121 BCE, of her elder son's in 133 BCE, or even from the time of her husband's death *c*.154 BCE, her withdrawal from the city of Rome was no modest widow's retirement. In the period after Gaius' death, Cornelia continued to attract and to entertain what we would now call celebrities.

It has become a truism of Roman (any?) historiography that women figure – if at all – in the historical record in connection with the men of their families. Cornelia is better served in the sense that many sources mention her in diverse contexts and *genres* but her image, as we shall see in chapters 4 and 5 below, was somewhat sanitized to conform to an appropriately feminine 'look'. Most later references to her concentrate on her role as the widowed mother devoted to the education of her young sons or the imperturbable bereaved mother bearing the death of those sons with exemplary fortitude.

One might have thought their deaths had put an end to Cornelia's ambitions, but her sons had left children to be brought up (Astin 1967: 319–321). Being fatherless, these children were likely to be educated by their paternal grandmother and aunt, particularly if their mothers remarried and even more particularly if their grandmother were already famous for her own intellectual and educational abilities. The political strategies of leading Roman families were long-ranging. Premature death was a setback, to be sure, but – like the death of a general on the battlefield – it need not mark the end of the war. Memories were long in these families. Descendants revered and maintained the reputations of distant ancestors. Personal ambition and family piety drove Roman nobles to pursue old feuds in the law court and the senate house.[30] The women of the families were excluded from direct participation in these public places, but they could be key players in the transmission of family honour and the maintenance of grudges and loyalties that would be played out in them. Cornelia had instilled political ambition in her sons. Now she and her widowed daughter Sempronia had yet more cause to instil both ambition and a desire for vengeance in the next generation.

Plutarch's highly coloured account of Gaius' last days in 121 BCE has his wife Licinia appeal to Gaius together with their child (*paidion*, singular). When he persists in his intention, she collapses and is taken (presumably with the child) by their servants to her brother's home, in anticipation of the devastation that was about to visit their household (Plut. *GG 15*). Tiberius' contemporary Sempronius Asellio wrote of Tiberius Gracchus towards the end of his life, addressing the *concilium plebis* in tears, committing himself and his children to their care and he adds that Tiberius actually displayed his only male child on that occasion.[31] Gaius is cited as referring *c.*122 BCE to the stock of Publius Africanus and Tiberius Sempronius Gracchus (i.e. his father) as now being represented solely by himself and a '*puer*' (boy), a term which could be used very loosely, especially in a rhetorical context of this type.[32]

Valerius Maximus' account (9.7.2) of the trial in 100 BCE of the former censor Numidicus provides another interesting element. As censor, Numidicus had used his position to challenge the civic status of the *popularis* tribune Equitius, who claimed to be the (illegitimate) son of Tiberius Gracchus. Numidicus was subsequently tried by *populares* for this act and allegedly stated in his defence that all three of Tiberius' *filii* (a term which could mean sons or children) had died. Valerius Maximus has him listing the circumstances of each child's death, presumably not in order, for one allegedly died in infancy at Praeneste, another, born after Tiberius' death (133 BCE), at Rome and the third in Sardinia on military service at an unspecified date. If this information is accurate, the youth who died in Sardinia must have been the male child Tiberius had shown to the crowd in 133 BCE and also the '*puer*' of whom Gaius had spoken in 122 BCE. This young man could have been reared by Cornelia. Most of the modern scholarly speculation has revolved around the date of his death and the likely date of his father's marriage.[33]

Gaius' child might have been a daughter. And it is even possible that there were other girls who survived – the Latin has some ambiguity. Being fatherless, she (or they) could well have been reared in the usual Roman fashion by their paternal grandmother and aunt. It is even possible that that child married and reproduced in due course. It would not be especially surprising that the sources passed over such an eventuality. We have seen how little interest the sources showed in Cornelia's sister and daughter. And we have seen that daughters, who could not perpetuate their birth family's name in their children, could nonetheless instil in them a strong sense of their heritage and their responsibility to it. So we can go on speculating about the daughter(s) and grandchildren of the Gracchi.

Although we hear from later sources of Cornelia's behaviour in her old age (Plut. *GG 19*; Sen. *ad Helviam 16.5–6*; *ad Marciam 16.3*) the references are not linked with dateable, specific incidents. The period 110–100 BCE marked a resurgence in the *popularis* cause which had suffered such a set-back with the death of Gaius. The tribunes Saturninus and Glaucia and the political outsider Marius were in the ascendant at a time of great military crisis. There was also rearguard action from powerful *optimates*, such as that enemy of Scipio Aemilianus and of the Gracchi brothers, Metellus Numidicus, whose four sons lived to further his family's ambitions. These optimate–*popularis* battles, like most political struggles, were waged with symbols and propaganda as well as elections and military commands. Many of the incidents and sayings which have come down to us in connection with Cornelia and the Gracchi probably belong to this period. Which brings us to the controversy about Cornelia's famous letter(s) to Gaius. Two fragments of letters purporting to be written by Cornelia to her son Gaius, apparently around 123/122 BCE, eventually surfaced in some manuscripts containing the meagre remnants of the once-voluminous body of work by Cicero's contemporary, Cornelius Nepos (c.110–24 BCE).[34]

Cicero's allusion in the mid-first century BCE to Cornelia's prose makes it clear that her letters were well known to cultivated Romans of his generation: 'We have read the letters of Cornelia, mother of the Gracchi. Her sons (children) seem to have been enveloped in her conversation as much as in her lap' (Cic. *Brutus* 211).[35] The *Brutus* was a didactic dialogue about styles of Roman oratory peopled by Cicero himself and his two friends Brutus and Atticus.[36]

The surviving Cornelia fragments have several points of interest for modern readers, not least their content. The general tone of the letter fragments is rhetorical. That tone becomes increasingly recriminatory. The author wishes to dissuade Gaius from standing for the tribunate because, she argues, his vengeful programme will cause yet more anguish to their family, to the state and to herself. The fragments are in two segments, whether from one or two letters is not clear:[37]

> *First passage* You say that exacting revenge on one's enemies is a beautiful thing. Nobody could find it a greater or more beautiful prospect than I would, but only if it could be managed without harming the republic. But, given that *that* is not achievable, our enemies will have to go on prospering overall for a good while yet. And better that they stay unharmed than that the state collapse in flames and ruins.

> *Second passage* I would be prepared to take my oath that, apart from the murderers of Tiberius Gracchus, no enemy has caused me as much trouble and pressure as you have because of these schemes; and you should be going out of your way to take the place of all the children I had before and to ensure that my miserable remnant of old age should be as free of worry as possible. You should really want to make it your

business to see that whatever you do should be done with my approval. You should think it an abomination to undertake any major project against my wishes, especially when I have so little of my life left to live.

Can't you even leave that brief interval free of your defiance of me and your agitation against the republic?

What end will there be to it all? Will our family ever come to its senses? Will there ever be any tempering of that politicking? Shall we ever stop getting and giving grief? Will you ever be ashamed of catching the state up in turbulence and strife?

At least, if you really cannot stop yourself, stand for the tribunate when I'm dead! As far as I'm concerned, you can do what you like when I'm past caring.

When I'm dead, you will perform my rites and call upon me as your guardian spirit. When that time comes, won't you be embarrassed to ask for the blessings of the family spirits you neglected and forsook when they were alive and with you in person?

I pray that Jupiter may keep you from persisting in this course and get this absolutely idiotic plan instantly out of your head.

And if you *do* persist, I fear that you will, through your own fault, suffer such hardship throughout your life that you will never be able to live with yourself.

Experts have always been divided on the authenticity of these letters. More recent scholarship has shifted the focus from either/or issues of authenticity to a more complex analysis of the content and purpose of the fragments.[38] Coarelli (1978) has argued and Horsfall (1987, 1989) and Barnard (1990) have cautiously conceded the possibility that these letters, which apparently originate in the second century BCE, might represent genuine extracts from letters by Cornelia which were subsequently doctored and circulated for propaganda purposes in the bitter battles for the 'hearts and minds' of Roman voters some time between 110–100 BCE.[39] Instinky's analysis established that the letters were *optimate* propaganda, replete with political buzzwords.[40] This reading accords with the conclusion I had reached from other scattered references in the sources, that Cornelia's name was politically significant and that it was worthwhile for family enemies to spread the notion after her younger son's death that she had not approved of his politics. She was thus converted into a less successful Volumnia type, who had tried but failed to avert her son from his destruction of his native state. Like everyone else, I would be delighted to have some trace of Cornelia's voice but I am now persuaded that, as they stand, these fragments are at best perverted versions of something she might have written.

Cicero's is the earliest reference to her letters. Imperial authors took up the theme. Quintilian (*c*.40–113 CE) invokes the letters in his work on oratory:

> We have heard that much of the eloquence of the Gracchi was the work
> of their mother Cornelia, whose most cultivated prose has been handed
> down, through her letters, to succeeding generations.[41]
>
> (Quint. *Inst.Or. 1.1.6*)

It is possible that Quintilian based this remark on Cicero's comment above,
rather than on first-hand knowledge of the letters. But, whatever the basis of
their information, it is notable that these sources do not associate the letters
with reproof of Cornelia's sons or in any other way suggest the withdrawal
of her support for either son at any stage.[42] In fact, Plutarch's reference to
her letters ('For this was written in code in her letters to her son'), apparently
drawing on an historic source rather than on letters he has seen,[43] ties her to
Gaius' political activity in the 120s BCE, for it includes the allegation that
she sent hired thugs from the country to help him in Rome. The accusation
(which could well have been true) seems to have been part of a tradition
hostile to Cornelia *because* of her firm support for Gaius. It is of a piece with
other traces of political criticism of her dating back to that period.[44] By the
last decade of the second century, the cult of the dead Gracchi was part of
the *popularis* resurgence and Cornelia's name, while still useful to both sides,
was no longer assailable.[45]

I, too, believe that the letters as we have them represent optimate propaganda, probably dating to the late second century BCE, rather than much
later schoolroom rhetorical creations – which is what I had initially assumed.
I have no suggestions to offer as to why or how they showed up in a manuscript with works by Nepos. But I do have an observation and a suggestion
to add to the accretion of speculation. The observation is that the first
passage seems quite different from the second. The suggestion is that it could
have been taken from a letter urging caution or change in a specific course
of action. Why not the motherly intervention which Gaius (Plut. *GG 4.3*)
gave as his reason for withdrawing his pursuit of their enemy Octavius
through tribunician legislation? Perhaps Cornelia did actually intercede on
this issue. Or perhaps it simply suited Gaius to make her his pretext for
abandoning a dubious strategy.[46] The argument of the first passage is quite
sympathetic to Gaius. It provides a face-saving rationale for postponing the
'beautiful' aim of revenge in favour of lofty principles, reasons of state and
the greater good (rather than the more likely reason of not securing the
numbers to ensure the promulgation of the bill). It could therefore have been
a genuine letter or a piece of propaganda circulated by Gaius' supporters –
including his mother, who would surely have been well able and willing to
furnish a convincing piece of prose perhaps longer than the truncated version
we have.

The second fragment is quite different. It paints Gaius unambiguously
as a reckless political character careless of the good of his state or his dear
old mother. Why his dear old mother would not want him to stand for the
tribunate is mysterious and at odds with everything we know of Roman

nobles in general and of Cornelia in particular.[47] Leaving aside the stylistic issues and emotional elements, this second passage reads very much as something written some time after the event, to blacken not only Gaius' name but the names of those who used him as a rallying point for their cause. Which brings us back to Cornelia's role, as actor or symbol, in the propaganda wars of 110–100 BCE.

We are told that Cornelia lived to be an old woman – but since she was in her sixties by the time of Gaius' death, that in itself is little help in fixing the date of her death. We know from Sempronia's appearance at a highly publicized lawsuit in 101/0 BCE that both she and the myth of her brother Tiberius Gracchus were alive then – over thirty years after his death – and that Cornelia probably was not. Or not in the flesh. The circulation of the 'Letters to Gaius' implies that both Cornelia and her dead son Gaius were valuable symbols which could be manipulated in these propaganda wars – as Gaius had invoked the name of his living mother and his dead brother in his oratory decades earlier (Plut. *GG 4,5*; *ORF 183, 197ff.*).

Plutarch wrote that humble supporters of the Gracchi, cowed at the time of Gaius' pursuit and death, were seized 'a little while later' by remorse and went out of their way to express their appreciation of the two brothers:

> They had statues constructed and set up in public and treated the sites of their deaths as holy, bringing seasonal offerings there. Many people made daily sacrifices and offered devotions as if on a visit to places of holy pilgrimages.
>
> (Plut. *GG 18.3*)

He also records Cornelia's approval of these rites as 'fitting monuments' of her dead sons (Plut. *GG 19.1*). All of this suggests that she and other family members, such as Sempronia and perhaps relatives of the Gracchi children (even after the deaths of those children), kept alive the memory and meaning of these deaths. We cannot date this martyr-cult specifically. It might not have been safe – or even possible – to pursue it until some time after Gaius' death, perhaps when the prosecution of Opimius signalled a rise in the shattered *populares* fortunes in 110 BCE.

From this great distance, it is difficult for us now to re-shuffle the scraps of evidence from undated (or deliberately misdated) sources, such as the letters. The vexed issue of the bronze statue to Cornelia is another awkwardness. Plutarch locates it in the early characterization of Gaius' oratory and his relationship with the common people, between the references in his speeches to Tiberius' unjust fate and those to his mother for, we are told (4.3–4), it was his admission in a speech that Cornelia's intervention had driven him to withdraw the legislation targeting Octavius that particularly pleased the populace:[48]

> Gaius himself withdrew the bill he had tabled, saying that his mother Cornelia had pleaded Octavius' cause. The people were touched and

delighted, for they honoured Cornelia on her sons' account as much as her father's and they [later] set up a bronze statue of her and [later] inscribed it: 'Cornelia, mother of the Gracchi'.

(Plut. *GG* 4.3–4)[49]

Since the erection of statues in public places to women ran counter to Republican Roman practice, many modern scholars have dismissed Plutarch's claim. But the context suggests a thematic rather than a chronological grouping. Plutarch, a Greek imperial subject writing his comparative Greek/Roman heroic histories in the late first century CE, treats the Roman people (*demos*) as a constant. There is no telling what he meant by 'later' (*GG* 4) or 'a little later' (*GG* 18). The appreciation of 'the populace' might well have post-dated Gaius' and even Cornelia's death and been part of the symbolic restoration that marked the end of that century.

Scholars have doubted that this could have been the same statue viewed by the elder Pliny which he describes as being in the porticus of Octavia, rebuilt by the new *princeps* (emperor or *tyrant*) Augustus from the original mid-second century BCE porticus of Metellus.[50] The scholar Coarelli (1978) has suggested that the pro-Gracchan *populares* provocatively placed Cornelia's statue there in an act of triumph over the optimate Metelli around 106–100 BCE. Given the traditional Roman resistance to the notion of public honorific statues to women, such a monument would be highly significant. Marius eventually broke from his patrons, the Metelli, and aligned himself with tribunes, in *popularis* style, to gain his spectacular military commands. Rekindling the Gracchan flame which Cornelia, Sempronia and their ilk had kept alight all those years might well have suited the plans of Marius, Glaucia or Saturninus. Reformers are often more useful – and less awkward – after their deaths.

The Metelli were, however, a strong force in the politics of the time, as is evident from their role in the rise of the great general Marius, the new *popularis* hero.[51] Metellus Numidicus achieved the censorship and proceeded to use its powers in the usual fashion, to serve his own political ends. He expelled the *popularis* Equitius from the citizen rolls. As we have seen, this arbitrary act was challenged by Equitius' political ally, the tribune Lucius Appuleius Saturninus, who prosecuted the censor in 101/100 BCE. Sempronia's appearance as a witness at that trial is extraordinary for it was not customary for distinguished women of her type to be subjected to the kind of bullying and public display associated with these highly public, politically motivated trials.[52] As one would expect from the granddaughter of Scipio Africanus and the daughter of Gracchus and Cornelia, she held firm. She insisted that Equitius was *not* the illegitimate son of her brother Tiberius. As he does from time to time, Valerius addresses Sempronia directly:

I do not include you, Sempronia, sister of Tiberius and Caius Gracchus, wife of Scipio Aemilianus, in a malevolent narrative with some ridiculous aim of implying your meddling in serious male business. Rather, I shall preserve your dignified memory because, when you were hauled before a gathering of the people by a tribune of the *plebs* at a time of great turmoil, you proved worthy of the distinction of your family. You were compelled to stand firm and endure the glowering of leading citizens, the pressure and threatening mien of a hectoring tribune, the cries of an importunate populace striving with all its partisan zeal to urge you give a kiss of kinship to Equitius, false claimant to membership of the clan of the Sempronii, as the son of your brother Tiberius. Yet you repudiated that creature that had been dragged up from some horrendous depth, and his false, atrociously impertinent pretensions to kinship.

(Val.Max. 3.8.6)

It is not easy to deconstruct the politics of this incident, passed on in Valerius' characteristically silly way. Tiberius had been dead for over thirty years so Equitius must by then have been on the citizen rolls for decades. His claim to a relationship with Tiberius Gracchus would surely have more to do with contemporary political battles and symbols than his basic rights as a Roman citizen. The detailed meanings – of his claim, of his expulsion by Metellus, of Sempronia's testimony publicly exonerating Metellus of a criminal charge – are impossible to disentangle at this distance. It need not mean that she aligned politically with the optimate Metellus against her brothers' political heirs, the *populares*. The unanswerable question must join other puzzles of this volatile and impenetrable period of politico-familial alignments and issues: Gaius' military service at Numantia under his brother-in-law after the falling-out between Aemilianus and Tiberius; the pro-Gracchan Mucius Scaevola's alliance by marriage with the daughter of the anti-Gracchan Laelius; the alleged location of the seated bronze statue of Cornelia, 'mother of the Gracchi', in a porticus devoted to the celebration of their enemies. Sempronia's court appearance as the authoritative representative of her birth family is generally taken as evidence that Cornelia had died by 101–100 BCE, but it is just possible that she was alive but too infirm to make the trip to Rome. If so, she would certainly have been very old indeed by then, at least in her eighties. It is more likely that Sempronia had outlived all of them, including Tiberius' and Gaius' male children.[53]

Plutarch's relatively detailed accounts of Cornelia's active 'old age' are likely to have originated with Sempronia or with some other close family member or loyal dependant. Sempronia's politics as such are uncertain, but her heritage ensured her loyalty to the memory of her brothers and of Cornelia. The brothers' *philotimia* – literally, love of honour – is attributed to their mother (e.g. TG 8.7, GG 4).

Women's ambitions in the ruling nobility at Rome – as at so many places and times – had to be channelled through their menfolk. Granddaughter, daughter and widow of three of the century's greatest generals, Sempronia was herself elderly and distinguished by the time she made her last public

appearance in the historical record. With the *popularis* revival, her brothers'
memory once more gained political currency, and she was uniquely placed
to promote them and their mother. One would expect no less of the sister of
the Gracchi and daughter of Cornelia.

3 Culture wars

Youth going to pot

Indeed, the decadence of the young men's behaviour in their pursuit of pleasure had got so out of hand that many were prepared to pay a talent for a *delicium* (boy-favourite) and plenty would pay 300 drachmas for a pot of salt fish from the Euxine. This was what Marcus Cato was alluding to when he said in his speech before the people that you could definitely see that a state was hurtling down the path to ruin when pretty boys fetched a better price than paddocks, and jars of roe more than ploughmen.

It became obvious that this sort of extravagance had got out of control at the period we have been considering, when the Romans judged their supremacy to be universal and absolute with the destruction of the Macedonian kingdom [168 BCE]. It was at that point that they made a huge display of wealth in their private lives and in public expenditure, after the royal treasures had been transferred from Macedon to Rome.

(Polybius 31.25 (24) 5–6)

The Second Punic War (218–201 BCE) was fought on the Romans' doorstep, with the Carthaginian army luring away their allies, dealing harsh blows to their morale and depleting the resources of the countryside. But *Tyche* – Fortune, a common theme of ancient historiographers – brought about one of her famous reversals. The long, hard-fought war, a time of sacrifice and austerity for Rome, was succeeded by triumph and almost immediate imperial expansion on an unprecedented scale into the eastern Mediterranean and north Africa, as well as the established Roman stamping grounds of Spain, Sardinia and Sicily. Wealth and slaves poured into Rome, chiefly into the hands of the ruling elite, who altered their style of agriculture, of display and of culture. Their vehemently competitive political style remained and they flung themselves into lavish public spending, vigorous opposition to enemies' triumphs, self-righteous prosecutions of corruption and expulsions of morally unsuitable opponents from the senatorial rolls.[1]

It was an exciting period, a true cultural revolution. The physical surroundings visibly changed as Greek sculpture and metal artefacts adorned public spaces, Roman temples were slowly transformed by more elegant materials and structures, and basilicas (advertising the key political families) became part of the urban scenery. Leading Romans enthusiastically embraced the Greek language and Greek studies like rhetoric and philosophy, while 'Roman' – that is, Italian – authors developed a whole new literature in Latin. The annalistic poet Ennius, the playwrights Plautus and Terence and the satirist Lucilius all belong to this era. Noble families took up such authors, as well as intellectuals and artists from Greece, and many nobles turned their own hand to serious literary work.[2]

Cornelia's father Publius Cornelius Scipio, named 'Africanus' in tribute to his conquest of Hannibal, was the most famous of the many great generals who had distinguished themselves in the long Punic War. He was also a leading proponent of the new style of luxury and culture, one of the first to associate the villa with a life of culture and contemplation.[3] His wife Aemilia, daughter of another great general, became famous for the splendour of her special equipage which her entourage of slaves carried for her performance of religious rites, to the admiration of other women:

> It was Aemilia's way . . . to create a magnificent spectacle whenever she set forth on women's religious processions as a mark of her part in Africanus' life and achievements at the peak of his good Fortune. Apart from her own clothing and the decoration of her wagon, all the implements for the ceremonies, including ritual baskets and chalices, were of gold and silver. And they were carried by her personal retinue as she made her stately progress in public at these festivals – not to mention a huge crowd of pages and maids who walked at the side and in her train on these grand occasions.
>
> (Polybius 31.26.3–4)

But, while many of the nobility embraced the new opportunities, others, who viewed change with genuine suspicion, or simply saw a good opportunity for tapping into the ever-present political seam of conservatism and xenophobia, represented the change in terms of cultural invasion and moral decline. Marcus Porcius Cato known as 'the elder' or 'censor', was the self-appointed guardian of tradition. He spearheaded resistance to the new-fangled culture and luxury which altered his world over the course of his long life (234–149 BCE). Unlike his great contemporaries – L. Aemilius Paulus, Ti. Sempronius Gracchus (senior), Publius Scipio Africanus the elder – Cato was not born into the political elite, but his undoubted skills secured grand patrons who fostered his career. By the time Hannibal had been driven from Italy, Cato had won military honours and become a political force. He attained the consulship in 195 and the censorship in 184, the year of Scipio Aemilianus' birth, when Cornelia was a little girl, probably being educated at home by Greek tutors who nurtured the literary and conversational skills for which she was to become famous.[4]

Scipio Aemilianus and Cornelia were thus children of the new era, fully bilingual from an early age in their reading and Greek composition as well as their speech. Both were dedicated and prominent supporters of the new style in all its aspects: philosophy, literature, cuisine and the visual and decorative arts. Given the choice of booty by his biological father (the great general L. Aemilius Paulus) at the sack of the wealthy seat of the Macedonian king in 168 BCE, the teenage Aemilianus went straight to the royal library for his loot (and which of us would not, dear reader?). By contrast, Cato boasted of his lack of Greek and manufactured a public *persona* which exaggerated his rusticity and made a virtue of his relatively humble origins. Of course, he was not an uneducated man, but rather an impressive public speaker, a wit and an author of whom it has been said that 'Latin prose was his own creation'.[5] In his political feud with the Scipios (initially pursued in league with Cornelia's future husband Tiberius Sempronius Gracchus senior), Cato employed the language of moral warfare.[6] The charges of corruption, decadence, effeminacy and 'Greek living' which he directed against Cornelia's father Africanus and her uncle Lucius Scipio were to be recycled to other enemies and generalized to a Roman society under cultural siege from its military conquests.[7]

Cato's speeches and sayings were not the sole reason that the theme of moral decline became so firmly embedded in Roman oratory and literature. All change is unsettling and these developments took place against continuing manpower demands on the populace for foreign warfare, combined with pressures on small-scale farming. Political battles over military service and the right to land grants and citizenship grades were interspersed with intermittent attempts to regulate cultural and moral change. Throughout this century, anxieties sparked intermittent overreactions to such targets as 'foreign' religions, theatre, philosophy, extravagance and women's access to property and status symbols.[8] These trends, too, set the tone for future ages. Even in the first century BCE, when study in Athens or Rhodes became a normal stage in the education of elite Roman youths, ambivalence about Greek culture and defensiveness about the contemplative or intellectual life permeated Roman literature.[9] The juxtaposition of the contemplative versus the active life, luxury versus austerity, Greek learning versus traditional Roman/Italian culture was played out in many venues. Cato on the one hand and Aemilianus and Cornelia on the other are convenient devices for this discussion here.

Accusations of decadence and praise for old-fashioned austerity become commonplace in Roman political life from this period – and Greek rhetoricians trained Roman nobles well in expressing the sentiments in the most persuasive and entertaining way. Cornelia's father Scipio Africanus was accused of vaguely dissolute behaviour at the siege of Syracuse in 205 BCE and the slur was revived twenty years later.[10] Posterity has kindly preserved many of Cato's own assertions about the simplicity and purity of his lifestyle (Plut. *Cat.mai. 4.5–6, 14.2*; Aul.Gell. *13.24.1–2*). Polybius' adulatory portrait of his friend Scipio Aemilianus, echoed by Cicero, paints him as a man of great culture (which he was), a successful warrior (which he was) and a clean-living soul with modest tastes (hmmm).[11] His biological father Lucius Aemilius Paulus was even better served by a battery of sources that agreed he was a model of restraint in the face of temptation, to be classed with past symbols of propriety like Aristides the Athenian and Lysander the Spartan.[12] From now on, in senatorial and judicial debates, it is one's enemies who practise extravagance, gourmandizing excess and general impropriety.[13]

Fortunately for those of us who have more interest in legal, social and economic history than in battlefields, the disparate mass of information thrown up by the second-century BCE Roman cultural explosion casts interesting (if intermittent) light on women, including Cornelia and her mother Aemilia. This is not as strange as it might seem at first glance. The chronicles we have are overwhelmingly of the doings and motives of the ruling group, a highly competitive body always on the lookout for more ways of generating that mathematical dynamic whereby one's own honour is advanced at the expense of a rival's. We have already seen that the new wealth and culture provided new discourses for this eternal contest. Clients, slaves, soldiers, foreigners and authors could be caught up in the conflict – why not women? Masculine pride converts readily to boasts of a wife's virtue, the display of wealth on her person or 'complaints' about the size of a daughter's dowry. The repeal in 195 BCE of a wartime restriction on the use of gold and purple by Roman women was the occasion of a well-organized female demonstration. Livy included in his account (34.1–8) his version of the debate between the tribune who proposed the repeal (on the grounds that its *raison d'être* no longer applied to the newly prosperous post-war Rome) and the consul, Cato, who argued in vain that the restrictions should remain in force. Cato's conservatism was also evident a generation later in his speech – of which a few fragments survive – in support of the *lex Voconia* of 169 BCE which regulated aspects of inheritance and made it illegal for any testator (or testatrix) in the top census class to institute a woman heir to a will.[14] Whatever the intention and precise content of that much-discussed statute, it patently failed to prevent high-ranking Roman women from acquiring, managing and disposing of substantial property, including real estate.[15]

In the early second century, it was the norm for Roman women to pass legally on marriage from the personal control of their fathers into the 'hand' (*manus*) of their husbands and therefore to have no formal legal access to property ownership or management until widowed. By the late Republican period, the alternative marriage form (which had existed for centuries) had become more usual, and most married women remained members of their birth families after marriage. This shift also reinforced the tendency for women of means to make wills, to ensure that their children inherited from them rather than their siblings.[16] I have published extensively on the changes in marriage and testamentary custom underpinning the relative economic freedom which Roman women enjoyed in spite of the apparently restrictive framework of traditional Roman legal institutions, like the extreme powers (*patria potestas*) vested in the male family head (*paterfamilias*) and the lifelong 'guardianship' of women (*tutela mulierum perpetua* – Dixon 1984). Here I shall instead follow the Roman lead of using personalities to display the rhetorical categories. This suits my focus on Cornelia and her family, who provide excellent examples for my purposes, just as they did for the very different purposes of the ancient authors who dished them up for my cannibalization.

It is not a coincidence that the enormous dowry of fifty talents bestowed on each of Scipio Africanus' daughters and the opulent display by his wife Aemilia contrast dramatically with the legendary austerity of Aemilia's brother L. Aemilius Paulus, whose assets had to be realized in order to repay his second wife's dowry from his estate.[17] All three examples have been passed on to contemporaries and posterity via what would now be called Scipio Aemilianus' publicity machine. The historian Polybius details Aemilianus' considered plan to establish a reputation for 'generosity and integrity', a plan which Fortune (*t' automaton*) fostered by timing the deaths of his adoptive grandmother Aemilia, then of her brother, Aemilius (Aemilianus' biological father), perfectly to suit his five-year plan.[18] On Aemilia's death in 162 BCE, each of her sons-in-law, Tiberius Sempronius Gracchus and P. Cornelius Scipio Nasica, was owed half the agreed dowry. Aemilianus was the heir to her estate, entrusted to pay out the large sum of twenty-five talents each to the two great men, both considerably his seniors in age and achievement. Polybius tells us that Gracchus and Nasica, who had gone to the banker to collect the first instalment, assumed there was a mistake when the full amount was handed over. And were confounded and abashed by Aemilianus' munificence when he informed them – in a public manner, subsequently made more so by the helpful Polybius – that he wished as Aemilia's executor to make this grand gesture, the second in a series related by Polybius (31.25–30).[19]

The first act of generosity which Aemilianus had exercised was designed to appeal to the women of Rome. The splendid accoutrements which Aemilia had paraded at festivals were passed on lock, stock and barrel to Aemilianus' biological mother, Papiria. One wonders how delighted Aemilia would have been to know that her former sister-in-law would enjoy being the centre of this acclaimed set. Aemilianus gained particular credit for this attention to his mother because she had avoided the great social occasions since her divorce many years before, being unable to cut a figure in keeping with her birth and high station. Women praised Aemilianus when they saw Papiria in the wagon, surrounded by gold and silver, rescued from the genteel poverty and obscurity which had been her lot for the last twenty years or more:[20]

She led a more subdued life than appearances would normally require for someone of her high birth. For this reason until then she had stayed away from the chief religious festivals, but now on the occasion of an important public holiday, she set forth with Aemilia's fabulous accessories and carriage set. The women gathered to make their vows recognized all of it as being the very same, complete with fittings, beasts and their drivers. They raised their hands in prayer on his behalf, calling down a shower of blessings on him for his virtue and generosity.

(Polybius 31.26 (xxxii.12).6–7)

A cynical reader might wonder why her loving son could not have helped her out a little sooner. Papiria died *c*.160 BCE, so she had a limited number of outings as the centre of attention. But Aemilianus had achieved his goal, as we now say. The story had been firmly planted among the leading women of Rome whose network ensured that it would spread, for 'it is women's nature to gossip and, once they've got hold of a juicy tidbit, they can't leave it alone'.[21] Unlike the reticent men, of course.

Readers might wonder how Aemilia came by such riches in the first place. The bulk of it was probably from her husband's military conquests. She came of a great family but her father had fallen at the battle of Cannae in 216 BCE so she could have inherited only a relatively modest estate from him and her mother, although Roman notions of 'modest' are somewhat flexible and even in that period of relative hardship and less showy living, the landed aristocracy would have owned estates and slaves.[22] It was the outward display of wealth, for example through more elegant buildings and unproductive land and slaves bought for their looks, which became the badge of the new style. As usual, Cato provides the guide, with himself as the desirable *exemplum*, with his comment that 'he acquired fields fit for sowing and grazing, rather than ones that needed sprinkling and tidying for show' (Plut. *Cat.mai.* 4.6).[23]

Still, much of Aemilia's wealth must have come from the conquests of her husband Publius Scipio Africanus, who lived to reap the benefits of his own strategic talents and the new opportunities presented by 'peace' at home and conquest abroad. Aemilia was probably her husband's co-heir with her sons Publius and Lucius Cornelius Scipio at the time of Africanus' death in 183 BCE, but the *lex Voconia*, passed in 169 BCE, would subsequently have prevented her from listing her daughters in her own will as co-*heredes* with her adoptive grandson.[24] The fifty talents passed on to her daughters so long after their marriages was probably an additional widow's life interest to facilitate the spread of resources within this wealthy family.[25]

Aemilia's luxurious display on women's feast days was the equivalent of the masculine triumph, when generals like her husband paraded their booty – human and mineral – before admiring crowds. That was the pinnacle of a Roman's career, an honour that had to be won on application by the victorious general to the senate proving that he had fulfilled all necessary conditions (e.g. a minimum of 5,000 enemy killed in a single battle) and it presented a great opportunity for obstruction by his enemies and the envious.[26] All triumphs were great public festivals, with a spectacular parade from outside the city limits, led by the general in special dress on a triumphal chariot leading his soldiers (who all received distributions of cash) and displaying the loot and conquered peoples through the streets of Rome and culminating in a ceremony of dedication at the Temple of Jupiter on the Capitol, where much of the booty was deposited for the state. Even in this period of great Roman conquest over wealthy Hellenistic kingdoms and city-states, a few triumphs stood out for their extraordinary lavishness and memorability, such as those of Scipio Africanus 200 BCE, when for the second time Africanus staged public 'Games' from his own pocket, of Titus Quinctius Flamininus 194 BCE and of Lucius Aemilius Paulus 167 BCE.[27] Many of Aemilia's slaves and the gold and silver they carried aloft might have had their first Roman outing on the occasion of Africanus' triumphs. We cannot know when she first put together her memorable show or how often it would have been staged, but in the forty years between Africanus' victory at Zama and Aemilia's death it would have served the purpose of showing off Scipio's military success and wealth to the world at large. Gall and wormwood to his enemies, especially those who, like Cato, had publicly expressed distaste for women who flaunted such status symbols.

Triumphs, religious processions and funerals – all could be part of a status display and the ever-present political competition for honours.[28] But, as we have seen, there were different ways of playing that game. Just as Cato could make a virtue of *not* being cultured, so others could compete for glory by pointedly avoiding material ostentation. We do not have an account of Scipio Africanus' funeral but a few extracts from Polybius' famous description of the (generic) Roman noble funeral ceremony conveys its public character and its impact on the Roman crowd:

> (1) Among the Romans, when a man of standing dies the cortege takes him to the Forum and he is placed on the so-called Rostra . . . where, amid a great crowd of the people, his son . . . or other suitable kinsman gets up before them and delivers a eulogy, dwelling on his virtues and life achievements . . .

> [SD: *After the burial they place his image in a special shrine in the public part of the house with other such images of dead ancestors.*]

> (6) They take these images out and parade them on official days of sacrifice . . . and whenever one of their relatives dies, they take them to the funeral, putting them on men who most resemble the ancestors in size and build. These 'impersonators' wear togas with the purple border if the ancestor was a consul or praetor, or all purple if he was a censor, and – if he had celebrated a triumph (or won some similar honour) – in gold. They all ride on carts, with the *fasces*, axes and other appropriate

badges of office . . . borne before them in procession . . . and when they reach the rostra, they all sit in order on ivory seats.

(Polybius 6.53: (1), (2), (6–8))

Plutarch tells us that the funeral of Aemilia's brother P. Aemilius Paulus aroused admiration because its simplicity, like the modest size of his estate at the time of his death, demonstrated his indifference to the wealth he could have seized when he conquered King Perseus of Macedon (Plut. *Aem.P. 18.35.5*). Again, this 'simplicity' is relative, for we know that his sons staged splendid gladiatorial games as part of the funeral (Polyb. 28.1–6). Perhaps, as so often, the point is to draw a contrast with other more ostentatious funerals, perhaps specifically his brother-in-law's funeral, which Aemilia and her sons would have arranged some twenty years earlier. At that time, they would have had particular cause to make the most of the opportunity the funeral provided to display Scipio's achievements, for he had withdrawn from Rome a year or two before his death, hounded even in his retirement by his political enemies and refusing to return to face their attacks. The funeral itself and then Aemilia's regular parades in the capital after his death would have constituted pious reminders of her dead husband's greatness, with a tinge of reproach for his ungrateful treatment by his fellow citizens – all of which fed Scipio Africanus' growing 'legend' and showcased her own wealth and standing as his widow. This recurrent exhibition, repeated at intervals marked by the religious calendar, was doubtless a source of considerable satisfaction to herself, her son and her daughters.

Hellenomania: rhetoric, philosophy and literature

The arrival in Rome in 155 BCE of the leaders of three philosophical schools from Athens caused a sensation. The distinguished heads of the Academy, the Stoa and the Peripatetics were chosen as prestigious ambassadors to the Roman senate and were successful in securing a reduction of the war indemnity imposed on Athens. Cato, then nearly 80, seems to have been in the minority with his misgivings.

Cato was already old when the philosophers Carneades the Academician and Diogenes the Stoic came to Rome as ambassadors from Athens. The most cultivated of the young men immediately rushed to their side and gathered to hear their lectures and admire them. . . .

Other Romans were pleased at this development, and looked with approval at the way their youngsters greedily seized upon Greek culture and spent their time with worthy men but Cato was concerned from the first at this passion for talk sweeping the city. He feared that the youth, by re-directing their ambition, would enjoy building a reputation for fine speaking rather than for a life of action and military accomplishment.

(Plut. *Cat.mai. 22.(1–5)*)[29]

His fears were only partly borne out. Unfortunately for the inhabitants of neighbouring states, Roman youths continued to seek glory on the battlefield but Greek culture became a fixture. Philosophers had inhabited the Greek colonies of Sicily and southern Italy long before this and some had made their way to the less cultivated capital from time to time, but this occasion was one which made a great impression and was referred to by Roman authors of later generations as a significant landmark in their cultural history.[30] It is notable that it was Carneades' speech which most impressed the youths and the senators and even inspired a back-handed compliment from Cato on the venerable philosopher's ability to win whatever he wanted with his persuasive oratory. The enthusiastic reception of Carneades' lectures and of his plea in the senate highlights the ability of most upper-class Romans to appreciate the finer points of Greek rhetoric and reasoning by this date, nine years before the sack of Corinth brought new artistic treasures to Rome – another cultural landmark. Cato's insistence on having Carneades' speech to the senate translated (by the senator and historian M. Acilius) was a deliberate political gesture.[31] The intermittent expulsions of philosophers earlier in the century show that Cato was not alone in his prejudices, but philosophy – like the theatre – was there to stay.[32]

Philosophy would continue to exert its appeal to successive generations and it became a literary commonplace that noble youths needed in the end to resist that appeal in favour of the active life of service which their position imposed. In practice, however, most Roman students chose the parts of the broad philosophical smorgasbord which most appealed to their ethos and found philosophers who were prepared to modify their teachings and requirements for this most powerful audience. Rhetoric and practical ethics were of far more interest to most of them than epistemology, physics, metaphysics and sense perception. Although the main philosophical schools (including Epicureanism, which was not represented in the 155 legation) all had their adherents, it was soon clear that Stoicism was the most popular and the rather pragmatically honed ethical principles developed by Diogenes the Babylonian, Panaetius and Posidonius were most to the Roman aristocratic taste. The ideal Stoic aimed at 'indifference' to the disturbances of life, such as ambition, greed and passion, but need not withdraw from the political fray to develop his virtue in isolation.[33]

Cornelia's interest in Greek culture is attested by Plutarch and reinforced by Cicero's more detailed references to the quality of rhetorical training received by her sons. This emphasis on the elite boy as potential orator pervades many of our sources and tends to consign other aspects of education to the background. The recurrent biographic theme of the good mother's cultivation of her son's speech and her moderation of his excessive interest in philosophy provide an almost incidental confirmation of the importance of speech and rhetoric and of the pervasiveness of philosophy in the higher studies curriculum which had become established by Cicero's day.[34] In the innovative second century BCE, the rules were still being worked out in leading Roman homes, the site of young children's training. Cornelia's children Tiberius Gracchus and Sempronia were probably both young when the three ambassadors from the prestigious Athenian philosophical schools arrived in Rome in 155 and Gaius was born soon afterwards.

But even Cato had encountered philosophers before 155 BCE and, for all his conspicuous insularity, had given serious consideration to his favoured proponents. It seems highly likely that Cornelia was familiar with current philosophical thinking by the time of this landmark visit. Her father's infatuation with Greek culture was notorious – Cato had tried to use it against him towards the end of the third century BCE. Both Africanus and his wife Aemilia were people of high fashion, proudly conscious of the figure they cut, ever ready to dispense their considerable wealth and prestige to protégés. Not for them the affectation of traditional simplicity in public. They arrogantly set standards which few could live up to. It seems only natural that they would have provided their daughters with the finest teachers, as well as uniquely lavish dowries. Cornelia presumably spent a good part of her girlhood at the Liternum villa to which Africanus retreated in the 180s. He is the first Roman we know of to associate villa life with leisure and the cultivation of the mind – *otium*. Cornelia's mother Aemilia outlived Africanus by twenty years and, if she spent much of her time at Liternum, might have provided a model for Cornelia's own socially active widowhood at the centre of an admiring circle in splendid surrounds. There is no reason to suppose that Cornelia's marriage deprived her of the kind of intellectual stimulation and opportunities that she had enjoyed in her father's home. Her husband Tiberius Sempronius Gracchus, who had famously addressed the Rhodians in Greek, seems to have favoured the same cultural trends.[35] Cornelia's choice of teachers and her supervision of her children's education all contribute to the image of a confident, well-educated woman, well able to take charge of whatever responsibilities came her way.

In assessing the influences on her son Tiberius, ancient and modern authors have considered the political leanings of his teachers. The Campanian Blossius, who left his native Cumae to study in the Greek world, was celebrated in his day for his intellect and later became known for his loyal support of his famous friend and erstwhile disciple, Tiberius Gracchus. The refugee Diophanes of Mytilene, a guest-friend of the Mucii Scaevolae, was another noted Stoic associated with Tiberius. Some in the ancient world blamed these thinkers for encouraging Tiberius in his political schemes (Plut. *TG* 8.6). More recently, scholars have reflected on the extent of their political influence on the Gracchi boys and whether Cornelia might have chosen them with their particular political philosophies in mind.[36] What has not been discussed is whether Cornelia herself was influenced by philosophy. Yet Plutarch's description of her imperturbability in the face of such overwhelming loss is replete with Stoic language and concepts. Seneca, himself a Stoic, typically advocated the benefits of philosophy as an alleviation of grief, for the Stoic philosopher located the usual causes for suffering (e.g. bereavement) in the greater scheme of things. This perspective enabled the wise man to cultivate a strong spirit as a kind of shield against life's adversities, which he could not prevent but could view in a rational spirit. He expressed regret that women such as his mother had not had the opportunity to develop this skill (*ad Helviam 17.3–5*). Even when he praises Cornelia for her exemplary calm and endurance, Seneca does not suggest that she might have gained some of her powers from philosophy. His description relegates her to the ranks of a great and noble lady, one of many in Rome's history. Yet his portrait of the bereaved Cornelia strikingly resembles that of the 'wise man' put forward by Panaetius, Posidonius and reappearing in the Latinized versions transmitted by Cicero and Seneca the younger. Compare Plutarch's praise of Cornelia as exemplifying the power of the truly noble spirit, predisposed by nature and cultivated by study, to rise above the normal standards of behaviour and to endure Fortune's worst afflictions.[37] Certainly the portrait in each case is in conformity with someone exposed from an early age to the Middle Stoa and to the philosophical offerings being tweaked during the second century BCE to allay any qualms which Roman nobles might have about embracing contemplation over political and military action. Seneca's turgid essay on why the wise man cannot be affected by the blows of fate is a classic Stoic exposition:

> If we concede that the ultimate sanction of oppressive laws and savage tyrants – death, which puts us beyond the power even of Fortune to torment us – if, I say, we approach that extreme threat in a calm and rational frame of mind, in the knowledge that death is no evil, we shall more easily be capable of enduring all the other misfortunes – losses, pain, humiliations, dislocation, bereavements.
>
> (Seneca (the younger), 12.3)[38]

Scholars tend now to shy away from assigning philosophical labels to elite Romans of this era. Scipio Aemilianus' well-known association with the leading Stoic Panaetius simply inspires more rationalization about why Aemilianus cannot strictly be termed a Stoic. But, granted that our evidence is insufficient to allocate a particular philosophical allegiance definitively to Tiberius Gracchus or to his mother, I would strongly suggest that Cornelia must have been conversant with the concepts and terminology of the Middle Stoa and that her famous imperturbability might have owed something at least to her educated understanding of what enabled the 'wise man' to rise above the vicissitudes of fortune. Why not the wise woman?

Villa life: *luxus* and *otium*

> Every now and then [Scipio Africanus] would give himself over to his studies, periodically leaving the crowded mass of people to draw into port as it were and enjoy his own company in peace.
>
> (Cicero *Off.*3.2)

> [Cornelia] herself continued to live in the region of Misenum, as it is called, making no change in her customary lifestyle. She was hospitable and kept a fine table for entertaining guests, and she was always surrounded by Greeks and intellectuals, and all the kings used to exchange gifts with her.
>
> (Plutarch, *Gaius Gracchus* 19.2)

Before the Second Punic War, the ruling families of Rome divided their residences between the capital and the country seat which was the source of their continued wealth, in a style favoured by many landed aristocracies throughout history. But this habit, too, changed after the victory over Hannibal and by the late Republic it had become more common for such families to buy up large estates in different parts of the Italian peninsula with an eye to profit and lease them out or sell them on pragmatically, without sentiment.[39] Another second-century BCE innovation was the development of a villa culture, whereby some country houses were viewed not just as farmsteads but as retreats from the irritations and distractions of urban political life. Speeches of the first century BCE denounce the decadent life of so-called 'pleasure villas' on the fashionable coastal strip north of Naples. It all depended on the purpose and perspective. An orator like Cicero might before a jury stigmatize as *luxus* what he would elsewhere term *otium*, a life of scholarship, thoughtful conversation and studious reflection. Some of his philosophical dialogues are set in villas because of these more reputable associations.[40]

Plutarch's description of Cornelia's civilized life on the Campanian promontory of Misenum gives us the prototype of the unproductive 'pleasure villa' as a seat of learning and civilized conversation. We do not know exactly when she acquired the villa or how but we do know that she had other family connections in the region. Many have read the Plutarch passage quoted above as an indication that she withdrew there after the death of Gaius in 121 BCE, but it is more likely that it was her primary residence from the death of her husband Tiberius *c*.154 BCE.[41] Even before she made the villa her base, she and her husband probably visited it together at certain times of year and it would have been a pleasant retreat for Cornelia during his many absences abroad. Against the idea that she moved there after Gaius' death is the anecdote depicting her encounter when her children were small with a superficial 'Campanian woman':

> While visiting Cornelia, mother of the Gracchi, at her home, a Campanian woman (*Campana matrona*) kept showing off her jewels, the finest of that era. Cornelia put up with her chatter until her children came home from school, then said, '*These* are *my* jewels.'
>
> (Valerius Maximus 4.4 *pr*)

The recycled story is full of holes. These princely children certainly did *not* go off to a school away from home, and surely nothing but awe at Cornelia's

status would have stopped a tactless and loquacious neighbour from pointing out that Cornelia was scarcely a stranger to jewels. It is just possible that
the 'Campanian matron' represents one of those little local touches based on
reality, so often supplied by storytellers to give credibility to an old chestnut
reapplied to named contemporaries.[42] More to the point, one of the learned
men she engaged to teach her children was Blossius, an intellectual from the
Campanian town of Cumae. Blossius had studied under the leading Stoic
Antipater of Tarsus, who had dedicated a book to him, so his philosophical
credentials were impeccable. His political views were thought to be radical
and Plutarch tells us that 'some people' (which usually means a particular
author or orator) blamed Tiberius' politics on his teachers or associates, particularly Blossius and Diophanes, both Stoic philosophers. Certainly Blossius
was a political supporter of his student, friend and patron, Tiberius. We have
several versions of Blossius' interrogation by the former consul Laelius (also
a Campanian, probably from the elite of Puteoli)[43] in the aftermath of
Tiberius' assassination. Blossius subsequently left Italy.[44]

D'Arms's 1970 study of villas in the coastal Campanian region known to
Greeks and Romans as the 'Crater' contrasts the fortified villa at Liternum
to which Scipio Africanus withdrew permanently in the 180s (Liv. 38.52.1)
with the elegant villa which his widowed daughter Cornelia later graced
at Misenum. The description of Cornelia's lifestyle makes it likely that her
villa was one of the new 'smart' ones (*villae expolitae*) to which Cato
referred scornfully in a speech *c*.152 BCE and which Scipio Aemilianus
admired as 'most exquisitely adorned' (*expolitissimae*).[45] Her father's villa
at Liternum had also been a centre of study and refinement and was probably
her mother's primary residence in her widowhood. One would expect
the high-living Aemilia to have redecorated in the current fashion, but the
Liternum villa clearly struck Seneca more than two centuries later as quaintly
functional:

> I saw a villa built of square-cut stone, a wall surrounded by forest, and
> defensive towers rising up on both sides of the villa, as well as a cistern
> underneath the building and greenery, large enough to service an army!

> (Seneca *Ep.Mor.* 86.4)

Perhaps it was the cistern which enabled Seneca to soak in a bath in the villa
while musing on the great figures of the distant past who might also have
enjoyed this amenity. His vision of Scipio Africanus relaxing while he
scrubbed off the dirt of his rustic labour might have been unduly romantic.[46]

Cornelia's cousin and son-in-law Scipio Aemilianus and his great friend
Laelius also had Campanian properties, so her daughter, married to
Aemilianus, would also have been in the area at the same time.[47] Certainly
we get the impression that there was a great deal of social exchange in this
region within fairly easy reach of Rome, where public land had been sold off

Figures 3.1 and 3.2 Misenum as it is now. Cornelia's villa was somewhere in this area. Picture courtesy of Amm. Domenico Carro (www.romaeterna.org).

at good prices in the later years of the Second Punic War. Incidental references in our sources to villa life are scattered, inconclusive and often lacking detail, but some things are clear enough. The well-stocked noble library, an established villa feature by the first century BCE, certainly had its firm beginning in the second century, when the enthusiasm of the Roman elite was matched by the opportunities created by conquest to take their pick of royal Hellenistic collections.[48] Cornelia's library at Misenum could well have been a draw for intellectuals and literary types.[49]

This coastal area south of Rome appealed to Greeks because of its more cultured, Hellenophile atmosphere, its undoubted beauty and its convenient ports. The philosopher Panaetius, credited with shaping Stoicism to Roman tastes, and the historian Polybius were both well born, and were both close to Scipio Aemilianus, with whom they could associate on near-equal terms. They must surely have spent some time at his villas. Polybius has left a record of his admiration of the coastal towns: 'they contain in that region the most celebrated and beautiful towns in Italy, and the people of Sinuessae and Puteoli, as well as the Neapolitans, cultivate the coastal area near them' (3.91.3–4).

The 'Greeks' whom Cornelia entertained in fine style probably consisted of social equals and those, like Blossius, Diophanes and Menelaus of Marathus,[50] who were the cultural celebrities of the day, something between retainers and friends. Scipio Africanus had socialized with Ennius and in Cornelia's generation the playwright Terence was on very friendly terms with Scipio Aemilianus and Laelius – and therefore, one imagines, well known to their wives, including Cornelia's daughter Sempronia. The satirist Lucilius, like Polybius, was also an enormous political asset to Aemilianus in building and maintaining his image.

It is no longer fashionable to speak of the 'Scipionic circle' or to use the term 'patron' too freely of relations between Romans like Aemilianus and their socially inferior literary acquaintances, but it was obviously the practice in this period for elite hosts to cultivate promising and well-established authors, both Greek and Italian, as well as the philosophers and rhetoricians who might teach the younger generation and provide continuing intelligent conversation and advice to their hosts. In his 62 BCE defence of the Greek poet Archias, who had emigrated to Italy forty years earlier, Cicero painted an interesting picture of the cultivated elite at Rome and in the coastal town where Archias had settled:

> Italia at that time [closing years of the second century BCE] was full of Greek arts and intellectual pursuits and these areas of study were pursued more vigorously then than they are now in the same towns. Nor were they neglected here in Rome, because the political scene was peaceful.
>
> (Cicero *pro Archia 5*)

The 'arts' to which Cicero refers in this passage were famously boosted by the sack of Macedon in 168 and of Corinth in 146 BCE. Many of the generals of the second century who celebrated a triumph, displayed and installed on the Capitol notable architectural and artistic treasures, but Memmius' stupendous haul from the wealthy and cultivated city of Corinth in 146 BCE was considered a landmark in the development of Roman visual arts. Public spaces and wealthy private homes in Italy were transformed in this century. It is interesting that Cicero links the fine arts in this passage with *artes liberales*, the intellectual and literary studies relevant to a poet such as Archias.

On his arrival in Italy towards the end of the century, Archias attached himself to various nobles. People like Archias sometimes had very long stays with their wealthy hosts. Panaetius lived with Aemilianus and travelled with his party for the whole of his lengthy eastern tour 140/139 BCE. As always, the sources tell us only those bits and pieces which interest them and are relevant for their purposes. For that reason, we know the names of only three individuals who stood in that sort of relationship with Cornelia, but Plutarch's description (*GG* 19) is readily generalized. There were also many leading Romans of the day with serious literary ambitions, who would have been likely to pay court to Cornelia for a range of reasons, social and cultural (like her fine table or library), along with her royal and intellectual following. They would have included political allies – or potential allies worth cultivating during the lifetime of her sons or with an interest in restoring and possibly exploiting their posthumous reputation. Plutarch's intriguing snapshot leaves it to us to fill in the details from tidbits we gather elsewhere.

Cornelia and her cousin Aemilianus were identified in their own time as leading proponents of the new culture, which expressed itself not only in learning and the arts but in spending, food, the outward display of wealth and all that made up the good life. Although both were admired in their day and firmly lodged thereafter in exemplary lists, neither quite fitted the conventional mould. Polybius tells us that the adolescent Aemilianus felt he was considered by many to be indolent, socially awkward and even backward for his station in life. Cornelia's learning and her Hellenism did not quite sit with dominant Roman notions of femininity and motherhood. In both cases, their images were fine-tuned in their own day and progressively tamed afterwards to conform more readily to the stock virtues expected of noble historic icons. Both were still mentioned for their cultural contributions, but in time Aemilianus became typed as yet another great Roman general and Cornelia as a model mother whose Latin somehow eclipsed her undoubted dedication to Greek rhetoric, learning and philosophy.

4   The icon

'Wife, either fit in with my needs or get out!

When Hector straddled his wife like a horse, the Trojan slaves used to masturbate outside their door. And the modest Penelope always used to grip her husband where it counted, while he snored the night away.

You won't let me have back-door sex, but the wives of Gracchus, Pompey and Brutus had no such objections, and everyone knows that before the Trojan Ganymede arrived to mix the drinks, Juno filled in for the boy with Zeus to serve his special customer needs.'

(Martial 11.104: 1, 17–20)

'Even if a woman were beautiful, well-behaved, rich, fertile, her halls packed with ancestral images, and more virtuous than a legendary Sabine woman . . . who could stand a wife who was perfect? I'd much, much rather have my little pocket Venus (Venustina) than you, Cornelia, mother of the Gracchi, if you're going to bring your massive pride along with your massive virtues and count ancestral triumphal processions as part of your dowry. Get out! And don't forget to take all your loot with you: Hannibal and old Syphax, captured in his military camp, and the whole of Carthage while you're at it.'

(Juvenal 6. 161–163; 166–171)

Cornelia's name became so standard in lists of exemplary women of the classical world that the subversive poets Martial and Juvenal used it for shock value. To suggest that it would be a *bore* for a husband to hear the impeccable Cornelia boasting about her noble birth, or to cite her inventive bedroom acrobatics as a model of conjugal sex was a startling and amusing poetic device that must have brought a yelp of horrified laughter from a Roman audience, used from infancy to hearing – and piously rattling off – these famous names.

Romans loved exemplary lists: of virtuous wives, of stern fathers who put the state before their personal feelings, of brave soldiers and of married couples whose love overcame death. Such lists circulated within families, regions and schoolrooms.[1] Authors and orators drew on these familiar examples, and modern scholars dissect the remaining instances, in spite of their sometimes dubious historical worth. My approach has often been to ransack the stories for what they tell us about dominant Roman moral values, while preserving a certain scepticism about their factual content.

Women were praised above all for being good wives and mothers. The virtues of wives mentioned most often in tombstones and literature are precisely those which Juvenal lists: chastity, good breeding, good behaviour, the ability to bear many children. Exemplary lists could include not only Roman wives, but Odysseus' faithful wife Penelope or even gods, especially the long-suffering Juno/Hera. Wifely virtues were defined from the husband's point of view. A woman who forgave a husband's indiscretions, or put up with him anyway and was kind to his mistress (like Cornelia's mother Aemilia), or refused to remarry after his death, could be included in a gallery of virtuous wives. In Valerius Maximus' handbook of examples for use by orators, Cornelia's mother is listed under 'Wives' faithfulness to their husbands' because she refrained from reproaching Scipio Africanus for his affair with a slave and, after her husband's death, freed the girl and married her to a fellow freed slave (Val.Max. 6.7.1).

Romans particularly enjoyed the touching tales of couples united in death, or of heroic wives who chose death because the husband had been condemned by illness or political circumstance. But devoted husbands figured, too. Valerius Maximus gives us Tiberius' story early in his chapter on 'Married Love':

> Tiberius Gracchus had a male and a female snake captured in his own home. Once informed by the *haruspex* that the death of the female snake would entail the immediate death of his wife and the death of the male, that of himself, he considered his wife's safety rather than his own and endured the slaughter of the appropriate snake in his own sight.
>
> (Val. Max. 4.6.1)

Valerius Maximus follows this anecdote with one about a lower-ranking husband who was determined to commit suicide once his wife died. In neither case are we given specifics about motive or about the wife who inspired such an act. This omission is typical. Because the stories conform to an expected format, we are supposed to read into each one the inference of great love, the high quality of the spouse lost, or the virtue of the mourning wife/husband.

We saw in Chapter 1 ('Fact and fable') that this much-repeated story was recorded by Gaius Gracchus and probably formed part of family mythology which the fatherless boy, grown to political maturity, could exploit in the public realm. In some versions of the tale, Tiberius' decision is presented as an outcome of the age difference between himself and his young wife,[2] but the anonymous author of the work 'On Illustrious Men' (Auctor, *Vir.Illust.*) attributes his sacrifice to his love for Cornelia:

and when two snakes had slithered out of the family sacral couch (*genialis torus*) and were in his house, [Tiberius sought advice]. Once he heard the response, that one of the owners would die, depending on the sex of the snake which was killed, he gave orders, from love of his wife Cornelia (*amore Corneliae coniugis*), that the male be killed.

(*Vir.Illust. 56.16*)

Plutarch begins with the age difference, then spells out the connection between Cornelia's virtues and her husband's choice:

But she did such a superb job of rearing the children and administering the estate, and was so perfectly behaved, so devoted to the children and so noble-spirited that men felt Tiberius had made the right decision in choosing to die instead of such a woman/wife.

(Plut. *TG 1.6*)

Juvenal's quote above contains, iconoclastically twisted, a very similar list of virtues. In his long work on 'Conjugal Precepts', allegedly sent as a wedding present to an unsuspecting young couple, Plutarch lists Cornelia more economically as one of several 'famous, inspirational women'.[3]

Cornelia's right to be included in the lists of good wives (or women) was probably enhanced by her refusal of a marriage proposal from King Ptolemy of Egypt himself . Whether this story is true and whether the king in question was Euergetes II interests me less than the significance of the story to those who read or heard it.[4] It appears at the beginning of Plutarch's *Life of Tiberius Gracchus* but in some ways seems to belong to the later section, towards the end of his *Life of Gaius Gracchus*. It is part of the image of Cornelia, a noble and well-connected participant and patron, conversing with and entertaining her high-ranking and intellectual guests. The king who proposed to her is, one imagines, one of the royalty who routinely exchanged gifts with her at her Misenum villa, close to the ports which welcomed traffic from Spain, Sicily, Sardinia and north Africa – all places with which her father or husband had strong connections, connections inherited and exploited by her son Gaius in due course. But at the beginning of Tiberius' *Life*, the proposal becomes part of the virtues of the young widow, reinforcing the celebration of her extraordinary feminine qualities – that is, her distinction, her virtue and her fecundity – which make her fit to be a queen. Her worth is shown all the more by her decision to decline this fairytale opportunity and to remain instead in Italy, devoting herself to her children's upbringing.

In this context, the decision consigns her to the respectable ranks of a 'good woman', like her reappearance in lists of noble widows, all mothers of great men.[5] Her decision is laudable for its dual implication, her faithful devotion both to her husband's memory and to her sons' (and daughter's) prospects and needs. The term *univira* came to be applied to such women, although it was originally confined to a woman who went as a young virgin from the power of her father (*paterfamilias*) into the hand of the husband (*manus mariti*) and predeceased him.[6] It is not clear whether Cornelia was admired in her lifetime for this decision or whether it became part of the general praise that attached to her as she turned into an icon whose virtues were assumed and whose inner life was not discussed. We have no anecdotes apart from the snake story about Cornelia's marriage or her feelings for her husband Tiberius. The focus of the later myth is on Cornelia herself and on her sons. Even Scipio Africanus fades into the background. Her distinguished husband, a dominant force in second-century politics, and the daughter who must have solaced her in her long widowhood, receive little attention.

Mater piissima: 'My children are my jewels'

Readers of my 1988 book, *The Roman Mother*, will be familiar with Cornelia's reputation as an exemplary mother, one of a litany of noble widows singled out for praise because of their vigilant personal contribution to their children's moral and rhetorical education. It should be noted that all women who figure in such lists were mothers of famous, high-ranking sons. Cicero twice refers to Cornelia in one work on Roman oratory:

> [sc. Tib.] Gracchus was educated from boyhood through the conscientiousness of his mother Cornelia and schooled in Greek literature. For he had superb teachers from Greece, among them – while Tiberius was still a youth – Diophanes of Mytilene, at that time the most eloquent speaker in Greece.

> We have read the letters of Cornelia, mother of the Gracchi. It is evident that her children were enveloped not so much in her lap as in her speech.

> (Cic. *Brutus* 104, 211)

The emphasis on speech and the mother's close attention to her children's education reflects the interest of authors like Cicero, Quintilian and Tacitus in the inculcation of rhetorical skills in young boys, a key element of the Roman educational curriculum by the early first century BCE. Their stress on early language skills is so familiar to moderns consulting this book that I should point out its relative rarity throughout history. It was not self-evident to readers in antiquity that the development of the very young child required special vigilance, or that the mother had any particular contribution to make to a boy's rhetorical capacity.

Rhetoric became a crucial tool of the politically ambitious in the late Republic. In his historical overview of Roman oratory, Cicero foregrounds the Gracchi brothers. They were among the first Roman orators to display before the popular assembly at the capital the full flowering of an education in which natural talent had been systematically nurtured by the best of Greek and Roman training.[7] With the change of government to an effectively monarchic system by the end of the first century BCE, the nature of politics gradually shifted behind a constitutional facade which maintained the fiction of continuity. Rhetoric continued to be a vital element of the curriculum, but many deplored the decline of oratory in the first century of imperial rule. Quintilian's treatise on the foundations of rhetorical education addresses this concept of decline and associates it with other decadent modern developments such as leaving the care of very young children to unskilled slaves with poor Latin. This is the context in which he asserts the importance of the speech and culture of those who interact with young children. His point is that they should ideally be family members, social peers of the children, rather than slaves and the other inferiors usually designated to perform this role. He makes a special point of informing the reader that mothers, as well as fathers, are important:

> In fact, it would be my preference that the parents have the highest possible level of education. And I do not just mean the fathers: for we have heard that much of the eloquence of the Gracchi was the work of their mother Cornelia, whose most cultivated prose has been handed down, through her letters, to succeeding generations.
>
> Quint. *Inst.Or.* 1.1.6)

In the same vein, the reference by (pseudo-) Tacitus in his *Dialogus de Oratoribus* to Cornelia's venerable example is offered as a comment on his own day concerning the general decline in youth, educational standards, oratory and women. He recalls to his audience the good old days, when women took their domestic roles more seriously. While he, too, concentrates on the deterioration of oratory under the empire, he explicitly links children's intellectual and language training with their moral evolution and emphasizes the importance of parents personally monitoring children's speech – and even their play – to guard against any impropriety: 'Thus we have heard how Cornelia, mother of the Gracchi, Aurelia mother of Caesar and Atia [mother] of Augustus oversaw their upbringing and fostered the potential of their sons, all leaders (*principes*)' (Tac. *Dialogus* 28).

Cicero was born in 106 BCE, around the time of Cornelia's presumed death, at the height of the *popularis* revival, when her own name and the names of her sons became rallying points. By the time Cicero was attached in his teens to the elderly legal expert Q. Mucius Scaevola, Roman politics had become even more polarized and violent. As Cicero relates at the beginning of his work *On Friendship* (set in 129 BCE after the death of Cornelia's son-in-law Scipio Aemilianus), Q. Mucius Scaevola ('the augur') passed on to the young man reminiscences tinged with family and political concerns, much as Cornelia had passed on her reminiscences to guests at her Misenum villa. Other passing references suggest that Scaevola's equally prestigious wife, Laelia (daughter of Scipio Aemilianus' great friend Laelius), together with his son, who succeeded him as Cicero's mentor, also passed on stories from the collective family memory. Cicero's later references to the Gracchi brothers as turbulent enemies of the Roman Republic were probably coloured by these recollections, *inter alia*. They supplied rich anecdotal detail for the works he set in the second century BCE, peopling them with characters known to these and other elders who informed his youth. Laelia's own slant was likely to be anti-Gracchan. Her husband's kinsman, P. Mucius Scaevola, consul in 133 BCE, had been a Gracchan supporter but seems to have wavered as opposition to them hardened.[8] Cicero's references to Cornelia are entirely laudatory. He gives her much of the credit for her sons' rhetorical success, without blaming her for the moral and political shortcomings which he regularly ascribes to them.

Mater dolorosa

> From the one family I shall produce for your benefit two Cornelias – the first one, a daughter of Scipio and mother of the Gracchi. She marked twelve births with the same number of deaths. And, not counting those that the state never experienced full-grown and never missed, she saw Tiberius and Gaius assassinated and deprived of burial! And even those who deny their political worth would admit that they were great men. And to those who offered condolences and called her unhappy, she said, 'Never shall I call myself unfortunate – I, who bore the Gracchi.'
>
> (Seneca *ad Marciam* 16.3)

Seneca's unfeeling (to our mind) attitude to Cornelia's loss of children who died young was not unusual for his day. The death of an adult child, particularly of a son, was seen as the worst kind of loss for a Roman parent. Literature and epitaphs record the recurring lament at the unnatural fate which condemned mothers and fathers to perform for their children the funerary rites which they had expected those children to perform for them one day. And in the case of Cornelia's sons, they had not only died, but died violently and suffered every kind of dishonour to their bodies, their reputations and their political achievements.

In a system with significant age differentials between husband and wife and in a period of continual warfare, long widowhoods were not uncommon. Nor was infant death. In both cases, the kind of emotion it was acceptable to display in public was fixed by custom. Most cultures have very limited tolerance for displays which exceed the conventional expectation. Throughout history, therefore, many have had to bear in isolation and silence the individual grief which can go with any loss, regardless of protocol or expectation. For that reason, we can only speculate about the sorrow which Cornelia might have felt at the deaths of her father *c.*183 BCE, when she was a small girl, of her mother in 162, when she was a young matron, of the many children who died young, or of the husband she lost *c*.154 after a marriage long enough to produce twelve children.[9] She wins her place on the honour role of grief because of the number of children she lost and because two of them were the Gracchi – and, of course, because she was the daughter of Scipio Africanus the elder, conqueror of Hannibal. The extent of Cornelia's bereavements would be remarkable anywhere, anytime, as would her dignified endurance of them. In the preceding chapter ('Culture wars') I expressed my view that Cornelia's dignity in the face of such loss benefited from the kind of philosophical consolation which the Stoic Seneca had recommended to his mother Helvia to support her through his exile and disgrace (*ad Helviam* 17.3). The letters of Cicero and Pliny make it plain that philosophy was thought to help a bereaved aristocrat endure the blows of fortune and its invocation was as commonplace in elite Roman society as the advice and comfort now offered to the bereaved from the stock of religious, proverbial ('time heals all wounds') or New Age consolations.[10]

Apart from the formal funerals of famous men, we know little about the rituals of death in Rome in the second century BCE. Letters of condolence which survive from later periods have a slightly reproachful, 'buck up and get on with it' tone not unknown in modern discourse. The rather critical response which Plutarch mentions towards Cornelia's calm references to her dead sons (see below) implies an expectation of more expressive responses. Cornelia generally received – at least from her supporters in the subsequent tradition – great accolades for her 'noble' ability to rise above the norm. Lists of those who had suffered extreme losses were consciously used as *exempla*. When Cicero's 30-year-old daughter Tullia died in 45 BCE, he was distraught and one way he dealt with this tragedy was to hunt down such lists with examples of parents who had lost adult children. It is clear that Seneca (the younger) had similar lists to draw on a century later and that such lists included anecdotal detail, such as Cornelia's response to those who called her wretched. They also included counter-examples of those who failed the test and buckled under misfortune, like Augustus' half-sister Octavia, whose only son Marcellus had died young. She remained in mourning for the rest of her life and could not bear to hear her sister-in-law Livia's conversation about *her* sons (*ad Marciam* 2.3–5).

Cornelia's determination to discuss her sons and her father served the political purpose of rehabilitating their memories. I suspect she did more than simply reminisce about them. Her daughter Sempronia, who survived her, would also have inherited this family duty, especially if all the children of Tiberius and Gaius died before they were able to reproduce. It seems likely to me that the kind of detail to be found here and there in the Cornelia stories comes from a family tradition, passed on by a close relative, connection or dependant. Whatever their source, these stories reinforced the image of Cornelia as an extraordinary woman who merited a place in the collective memory. Her place was firmly entrenched by the early second century BCE in popular lists of famous wives, famous mothers and of famous bereaved mothers who bore their grief with admirable imperturbability. As Plutarch put it:

> Her conversation about the life and habits of her father Africanus was a delight to her visitors and her own circle. It was a source of amazement to those who heard her that she could reminisce about the sufferings and achievements of her sons without tears or regret, telling their story as if they were heroes of old.
>
> iv) For this reason, some people thought she had become unhinged by old age or the weight of her ills and was de-sensitized by the vicissitudes of fortune. In this they merely show their own insensitivity to the great advantage to be gained from a spirit which, naturally noble, is cultivated by sound education, in overcoming any human misery, and that, while Fortune can often be overwhelming and may storm virtue's defences against its assaults, it cannot rob it of the power to endure them in a noble spirit under duress.
>
> (Plut. *GG 19. 3–4*)

Augustan Icon:domestication of a political *grande dame*

WORK OF TISICRATIS

CORNELIA, D[AUGHTER] OF AFRICANUS OF THE GRACCHI

CIL VI.31610[11]
(Inscription on statue base found on the site of the porticus of Octavia, 1878)

> like the [bronze statue] to Cornelia, mother of the Gracchi, daughter of Africanus the elder, publicly displayed in the porticus of Metellus and notable for its seated pose and its domestic sandals. This statue is now in the complex of Octavia.
>
> (Pliny ('the elder') *NH* 34.31 (14))

In Chapter 2, I discussed my reasons for accepting that there was a statue of Cornelia erected towards the end of the second century BCE, during the *popularis* revival, probably after her death. Coarelli, as we saw, believed that it was the same statue which Pliny the elder viewed in the Porticus Octaviae some time in the first century before 79 CE.[12] The location of this statue of a woman famously connected with both Scipios (elder and younger) and with the notorious Gracchi brothers, in a splendid second-century porticus advertising their enemies (the Metelli family) has inspired ingenious explanations, but its place in a new-look porticus erected a century later and named after the emperor's half-sister Octavia is more readily accepted.[13] The differences of opinion centre on whether the statue was already there or recast from scratch as a historical revival.

We know that, like its predecessor, the porticus Octaviae, begun some time in or after 33 BCE, was a showcase for great works of art.[14] From the second century BCE, art and public building had constituted important public statements about leading political families and Roman conquest. The politically revolutionary Julio-Claudian era developed these trends, using public displays on historic and moral themes associated with the new regime.[15] Lewis (1988) suggested that the unusually pithy expression 'Gracchorum', 'of the Gracchi', would make immediate sense if Cornelia's statue had been part of a display of famous Roman mothers, corresponding to the sculptural displays of '*summi boni*', great men from Roman history, which were scattered throughout Augustan Rome to inspire new generations.[16] The idea of a gallery of mothers would be in keeping with Augustan propaganda styles. In establishing his new government and attempting to found a dynasty, the *princeps* celebrated the women of his family and tied their promotion to his programme of moral reform which stressed the importance of what his political descendants now call 'traditional family values', with state encouragement of marriage and motherhood.[17] His Altar of Augustan Peace features a famous semi-relief of a maternal figure with healthy children and the fruits of Italy, to symbolize the peace, stability and prosperity for which Augustus took credit.[18]

Octavia had played an important role in her half-brother's violent rise to power. Augustus, a superb propagandist, constructed his sister's image as that of a devoted, wronged wife during his struggle with his opponent Marcus Antonius, to whom she was married.[19] Once he was established in his position as *princeps* he looked to the future. He had no son, but Octavia did. Her son Marcellus, married to Octavian's/Augustus' daughter, was marked out for distinction and Octavia herself was heaped with extra-ordinary honours matching those of Augustus' wife Livia (Dio 49.38.1; 49.15.4). The porticus of Octavia, like the theatre of Marcellus, celebrated these important family members.

It may seem odd that Augustus, who represented himself as the guardian of tradition, should have endorsed the 'revolutionary' Gracchi even in this relatively indirect way. We have seen that, in spite of some rehabilitation of their political reputation, the Gracchi continued to be viewed as seditious by some imperial authors. But there is no end to the ways in which symbols can be manipulated and products re-badged. Modern advertising exploits the irrational association between unrelated things: images of glamour effectively sell products (like ersatz 'coffee' which once had the most patriotic and long-suffering wartime consumers complaining). In Chapter 3 we saw that it could be politically useful for very wealthy Romans to cultivate a reputation for austerity. The big-lie technique was not a twentieth-century invention.

Thus Augustus, who established an unconstitutional monarchic dynasty by force, continually claimed to have 'restored the republic' and to represent the people of Rome.[20] In the lead-up to the disintegration of the republican system, the conscious revival of *popularis* methods from 70 BCE on, for which the resuscitation of the plebeian tribunate was a key political tool, provided the platform for the rise of Augustus' great-uncle Julius Caesar and therefore (after yet another civil war) of himself. Lifelong 'tribunician power' was one of the battery of reprocessed republican offices which the patrician Augustus not only accepted but retained (*RG 27*).

And perhaps we are worrying too hard at these details. We have seen, after all, that Cicero, more conservative than Augustus and a great denouncer of the Gracchi's political acts, freely admired Cornelia and her sons' oratory. It is an occupational hazard for historians to look too hard for explanations for things which contemporaries accept unthinkingly. Few dispute that Cornelia's statue was in the porticus Octaviae or that the inscription to her was there in Augustan times. We can accept the proposition that there was a second-century BCE statue of Cornelia and that it was probably the one which the elder Pliny saw in the first century CE, without accepting all the convoluted arguments put forward by Coarelli to support his contention that both the base and the inscription to Tisicrates were part of the original. In manuscript readings, the guiding principle is that the easier reading is the likelier one. Perhaps we should opt for simplicity and agree that the special genitive requires no elaborate explanation and that Cornelia, as a paragon of motherhood and a famous woman from relatively distant history, represented in a fine piece of sculpture, could retain her regal seat in a glamorous new setting. The origins of the statue to Cornelia are emphatically political but, like Octavia, she now served a new political purpose in this (politically and architecturally) refurbished location in her domesticated role (complete with home-loving slippers) as a symbol of femininity, motherhood and – via her father – of Roman supremacy.

Over time, Cornelia's qualities were tamed into a generic image of a well-born widow devoted to her children but capable of exemplary self-control in the face of their loss. Her virtues as a wife are usually assumed rather than spelt out – her husband's appreciation of her is seen as an earnest of her worth. Cornelia had been at the cutting edge of the Hellenophile cultural developments in her lifetime and even those who take a minimalist view of her political involvement and discount the tale of her wish to be known as 'mother of the Gracchi' would agree that she had a strong sense of family honour and of political ambition for her sons. But within a generation of her death, her culture and her vicarious political aspirations had been reduced to respect for her contribution to her sons' rhetorical education: providing the boys with a model of good Latin speech and good teachers. By Augustus' day she was admired as a great mother of great sons, her statue ensconced in the spectacular new public building devoted to one of the great mothers of the imperial family. She was thus associated with the virtues of the new regime as a larger-than-life symbol of the virtuous wife, widow and mother. If Coarelli is right about the sculptor, her statue base encapsulates also the Augustan tendency to play down the importance of individual Greek artists but, through the addition to her inscription, to emphasize her role as daughter of the great conqueror, Scipio Africanus the elder.

5   Afterlife

Cicero, a key source for this study, was born in 106 BCE during the *popularis* revival, around the time of Cornelia's likely death, and was killed on the orders of the *triumvir* 'Mark Anthony' in 43 BCE. Most of his historical and rhetorical treatises peopled with second-century BCE characters, and citing the Gracchi and Cornelia, were written towards the end of a life which had spanned *popularis* and *optimate* resurgences and falls, all characterized by cruelty, slaughter and retribution. Cicero's references to Cornelia as an icon of Latinity and Roman motherhood epitomize her transformation from a vigorous proponent of Greek culture and family prominence into a feminized, featureless figure. The transformation had taken place within a generation.

In her lifetime, too, Cornelia was not only a flesh-and-blood woman but a public construct, an amalgam of other conscious, politically driven constructions, some emanating from the mythology surrounding her father Scipio Africanus the elder and the cult of her sons, who became instant objects of adulation and invective. Politics and family being inextricably bound up in Rome, the stories were maintained within kin and patronage circles and it suited both sides to call on the Gracchan martyrs and their sorrowing mother in the *popularis* revival in the last decade of the second century BCE. These family legends outlived Cornelia herself and Sempronia, her daughter, who surely generated and maintained them wherever possible. Sempronia, herself neglected by history, is probably responsible for the survival of Cornelia's own legend (Petrocelli 1994: 60).

This rapid reprocessing of Cornelia should not surprise those of us accustomed in an age of 'globalization' to the elimination of savour from food, regional variation from language and ideas from ideology. From being renowned in her day for her lavish lifestyle, her culture, her prose and conversation, her familiarity with leading intellectuals and international leaders, this woman – publicly vilified by enemies and a rallying point for supporters – had within decades become a byword for loyal wifedom, devoted motherhood and good Latin – a user-friendly McCornelia suitable for use in any Roman classroom. Her vigorous and cutting-edge pro-Hellenism and her independent voice were lost in this generic simplification into inspirational womanly qualities.

She was cited for her fecundity and praised as a *mater dolorosa* who bore her appalling losses with exemplary Roman imperviousness rather than as a proud mother who embarrassed guests with her stubborn insistence on the credit due her controversial sons. Even her famous imperturbability was admired by Seneca in generic terms as characteristic of a well-born Roman mother rather than the outcome of those Stoic, or at least philosophic, principles which he commended to his own mother.[1] And this from Seneca, the Stoic, recruited as court philosopher by another powerful, political Roman mother, another strong-minded daughter of another famous Roman general, another prose author with an eye to posterity and burning ambitions for her son, who was to become the emperor Nero.[2]

Although Cornelia's conversation and letters continued to be cited for their *elegantia*, her excellent Latin is portrayed more as a motherly benefit than as a characteristic of an educated author. Its value was to foster her sons' oratory. Her cultivation, for the sons' sake, of leading models of rhetoric, either Greek or trained in the Greek world (Plut. *TG* 8.6), became secondary to this moralizing emphasis on Latinity. The possibility that her patronage had been influenced by their political and ethical philosophies was not even touched on at the time.

The Augustan appropriation of her image via the statue in the porticus Octaviae showed that she still had her political uses under a completely different regime. Above all, Cornelia had become a famous and exemplary mother of famous sons who could still be invoked in grand, historical terms, as martyrs of the *popularis* cause and the potential of the tribunate to champion plebeian will against the capricious excesses of the ruling nobility. Daughter of the conquering Scipio Africanus and mother of the Gracchi, Cornelia was a fertile and noble symbol of the finest of Roman patrician and plebeian history. She was perfect for Augustus' purposes, highlighting his commitment to popular sovereignty and his promotion of marriage and motherhood.[3]

Cornelia's Christian afterlife

The classical scholar is often at a loss to explain why some images and personalities from classical antiquity are revered by later ages. The process seems not only mysterious, but often perverse. The wealthy, rationalist courtier Seneca and the militaristic emperor Marcus (Aurelius), whose reign saw particularly savage persecutions of Christians, have attained near-saintly status in various periods, while the Hellenophile Nero is still 'remembered' for playing an instrument that had not been invented and lighting a fire at a time when the most hostile ancient accounts concede that he was absent from Rome. Such oddities make Cornelia's continued celebration seem reasonable by comparison. Christian authors who, like their non-Christian forebears, valued selfless devotion in wives and mothers, tacked Cornelia and a few other traditional wifely models on to *their* exemplary lists. Aelian considered her in the third century CE to be the Roman equivalent of Odysseus' faithful wife Penelope, and St Jerome (347–*c*.420 CE) grouped her with Lucretia and Porcia as women whose virtues equalled those of their husbands. More interestingly, in his letter to Furia on the evils of remarriage and the pointlessness of having children, Jerome cites Cornelia as an 'exemplar' for her chastity and her fecundity but also as an example of sorrow and disappointment, since being mother of the Gracchi clearly did not bring her happiness.[4]

Cornelia as continuing patron and subject of the arts

There are so many things we do not – cannot – know about Cornelia. Given her background and lifestyle, it seems likely that she was a patron of the visual and literary arts, but we do not have any concrete information on the subject. It is – barely – possible that she confined her enthusiasms to the Greek and hellenized intellectuals and people of culture (*philologoi*) who thronged her villa at Misenum. But later ages have seen her represented in a number of art forms, so perhaps, in this sense, her patronage of the arts and her inspirational value have been the most enduring element of her afterlife.

As we have seen, her statue at Rome suffered as many vicissitudes as Cornelia herself had endured in her own lifetime. We do not know for certain whether the original statue survived until Augustan times or was erected then. Nor was it safe once installed in the splendid porticus Octaviae, appropriately flanked by Greek and Latin libraries, for two serious fires damaged the porticus over the next two centuries, in 80 and 191 CE. The surviving statue base bears the marks of fire and we cannot tell for certain whether her statue was restored in any sense in the Severan repairs of *c*.203.[5] Most scholars accept that her seated statue as described by Pliny the elder was a type based on Pheidias' seated Aphrodite, which in turn influenced later portrayals of distinguished women. The type survives in one well-known statue which is often associated with Helena, mother of the fourth-century emperor Constantine.[6]

But Cornelia has outlasted Late Antiquity. She has continued to inspire artists – or, in many cases, to inspire patrons to commission works illustrating aspects of her image and legend. Image and legend themselves have changed yet again and, as before, it is difficult to discern just what it is that attracts later worshippers to the shrine. The saying, 'My children are my jewels', probably proverbial or commonplace if and when she ever uttered it, has become inextricably associated with her in post-Classical times. Artists have often depicted her, with her children, while the Campanian woman vainly shows off her inferior treasures. A random selection of works of art makes the point. The eighteenth- and nineteenth-century paintings seem to have been influenced not so much by the classical revival which made the Pompeian room an obligatory part of the European aristocratic

Figure 5.1 A post-classical representation of Cornelia: Angelica Kauffman's 1785 painting, *Cornelia, Mother of the Gracchi, Pointing to her Children as Her Treasures*. Courtesy of the Virginia Museum of Fine Arts.

house (Trevelyan 1976), as by the upsurge of sentimental and historic depictions of motherhood and other family scenes from the late eighteenth century (Duncan 1973).[7] Jean-Francois-Pierre Peyron's 1781 painting *Cornelia, Mother of the Gracchi* is a smaller version of a painting commissioned by the Abbé de Bernis. It includes a statue plinth, with the fragment MP GRACCUS visible. The 1785 oil painting by the Swiss painter Angelica Kauffman (*Cornelia, Mother of the Gracchi, Pointing to her Children as Her Treasures*) is one of the few which includes Sempronia. Either other artists did not regard Sempronia as a jewel or, like Seneca, they were unaware that Cornelia had three children who survived to be adults.

A marble sculpture group completed in 1861 by Charles Cavelier shows Cornelia with the two boys only, Gaius young and naked, Tiberius formally dressed, wearing a *bulla* and holding a papyrus scroll, typifying learning. A stained glass window completed by John la Farge in 1891, 'Cornelia, Mother of the Gracchi', was commissioned by the Harvard class of 1859 to commemorate members of the class who had fallen in battle. It forms part of a series of windows in the Harvard Memorial Hall, very much in the Augustan tradition of inspirational historic themes.[8] Clearly, one distinguished all-male group in the nineteenth century found Cornelia an appropriate *exemplum* for a display to a select audience.

Cyber-Cornelia: trawling the net

And still it goes on. The culture wars continue, new forms proliferate and Googling Cornelia throws up all sorts of excitements. No longer confined to high culture sites and beautiful pictures hanging on walls frequented by a select audience, the post-Classical Cornelia now – appropriately in a way – lives on in a range of prose tributes peppered with illustrations plucked promiscuously from every possible period. Readers might like to follow the links and readings provided by the many first-rate scholars and enthusiastic teachers who have generously placed their own lectures or teaching outlines on open sites. The free enterprise cheat-essay proliferates, as does the short encyclopedic piece which frequently maintains the tradition of Dio's Byzantine excerptors and the works on 'Illustrious Men' by a late and thankfully anonymous author. *Caveat discipula!*

Creative anachronism is also represented, most intriguingly in Nova Roma, which classes itself as a micro-nation, the 'spiritual heir to the ancient Roman Republic and Empire' which classifies past and present membership of Roman *gentes* alphabetically. See, for example, their *gens Sempronia* entries. Again, the purpose is exemplary, for, as the 'spiritual heir' to ancient Rome, Nova Roma is bound together by 'shared Roman ideals'. I pass this information on without further comment and without responsibility.

The dust has settled. Today the great names of the Cornelii Scipiones and Sempronii Gracchi echo oddly in the cyber-halls of Nova Roma. Sempronia, custodian of the two flames, remains invisible to most. Perhaps Cornelia has fared better. Life was not kind to her. Born to privilege, she outlived not only her older husband but eleven of her twelve children and several grand-children. Posterity has treated her more gently. In the late Republic, samples of her prose circulated and were admired for their form and sentiment, even by her sons' critics. She was held up as a model mother and wife for centuries and her statue, first erected by political adherents, venerated her memory. But the flesh-and-blood woman, who might have been difficult to live with, has been cut down to a one-size-fits-all model. The cost of survival has been the transformation of her image into a safer, blander symbol of motherhood, pride and suffering leached of any hints of excessive intellect, haughtiness or bloody-mindedness that could mar the reassuring feminine qualities which continue to exert their mysterious appeal on new generations of artists, readers and students.

Notes

Preface

1 R. Huggins and J. Huggins 1994: 1.
2 See, for example, Steedman 1989; Bell and Yalom 1990: 1–11.
3 Ferrier (1999). I confess to feeling envious (as Tacitus rightly points out, *invidia* is a universal vice) of her access to a range of writings (including authentic letters) by her subject, as well as personal testimony from surviving friends.
4 See below. I tend to follow the expert view of Nicholas Horsfall 1989, that the surviving fragments purporting to be from letters written by Cornelia to her younger son Gaius Gracchus are probably contemporary forgeries but that they may represent doctored versions of her own writing. I discuss this issue in Chapter 2.

1 Fact and fable: sorting out the sources

1 Biographer David Marr, 1996 at a seminar at the Australian National Library on the use of private papers for research and publication. In pointing out that biographers resort to the evidence of aggrieved parties, he was speaking of living sources. My work is at a greater remove, but much of our written tradition on the Gracchi and the Cornelii comes from Cicero and others who derived it in part from just such living sources.
2 The office of plebeian tribune (*tribunus plebis*) had been established in the fifth century BCE, during the Struggle of the Orders, as a means of protecting the plebeian masses from the abuses of patrician magistrates (see note following). The ten tribunes elected annually by the Roman *plebs* could propose laws to the popular assembly (*concilium plebis*) and had the power to veto many public acts, but by the mid-second century BCE, the exercise of these radical functions had been softened by convention (Polyb. 6.16 has an interesting but probably idealized contemporary picture; cf. Liv. 10.37). Tiberius Gracchus' tribunate 133 BCE changed all that.
3 The division of the Roman citizen body into patricians and plebeians had been highly significant in Rome's early history, when patricians monopolized priesthoods, legislation and justice, but by the second century BCE, this distinction was largely irrelevant. The ruling group consisted of both plebeian and patrician 'noble' families who intermarried. Plebeian or patrician status was inherited from the father.
4 Liv. 38.57.3–8; Aul.Gell. *NA 12.8.1–4*; Val.Max. 4.2.3. See Carcopino 1928: 47–56; Bernstein 1978: 29–30.
5 These attempts were spearheaded by Scipio's enemies, notably Fabius Maximus, Cato the elder and Q. Petillius – Plut. *Cat.mai. 3.5*; 18.2, Liv. 38.50–57 *passim*.

6 A commonplace pact in private has less currency as narrative and no obvious role for the more famous Scipio brother. In assessing the story, Livy observes that it could not apply to 'our' Cornelia's elder sister: 'It had been determined that the younger of the two daughters should be married to this Gracchus, for the elder daughter had certainly been betrothed by her father to Publius Cornelius Nasica' (38.57, set in 187 BCE). Each sister was called Cornelia, in the Roman fashion whereby citizen women all bore the feminine version of the family (gentile) name.

7 Plutarch (Plut. *TG* 4.1–4) and Carcopino 1928: 56 both point to the suspicious similarity this version bears to another, about the younger Tiberius' engagement to Claudia in the next generation. Another *topos*?

8 Plut. *TG* 4.3 cites the authority of Polybius. We do not have the Polybius passage.

9 And the fact that the final payment of her dowry and her sister's seem to have been arranged in accordance with her father's will (Polybius 31.26 and 27). The final payments were made after their mother's death in 162 BCE. See pp. 6–7.

10 Val.Max. 4.4 *pr*; Plut. *Phocion* 19.3; *Moralia 241D (Apophth. Lak. = Sayings of Spartan Women 9)*. See Hemelrijk 1999: 263. For the continuing association of Cornelia with this story, see Chapter 5, 'Afterlife'.

11 Since his father died either before his birth or when he was very young. See *Div.* I.36 (*ut C.Gracchus, filius eius, scriptum reliquit*) and II.62 (*C.Grachus ad M.Pomponium scripsit*).

12 The sceptical speaker in Cicero's fictive dialogue makes the same points a modern rationalist would make, suggesting that Tiberius Gracchus' death was caused by illness, not the release of the female snake. He also asks the obvious question – why should Tiberius have let either snake escape if he thought the consequences would be so grave (1.36)?

13 Barnard 1990: 383.

14 Polyb. 31.27.1–16. See Dixon 1985a and Chapter 3 ('Culture wars') for more detail.

15 Seneca the elder, *Quaest.nat.*1.17.8 and Sen. (younger) *ad Helviam* 12.6 follow the romantic notion that Africanus' daughters were dowered by the state, apparently a variant on Val.Max. 4.4.10, in which the senate refused the request of Cnaeus Cornelius Scipio (uncle of Cornelia's father Publius Cornelius Scipio) to return to Rome from his command in Spain to arrange his daughter's marriage. Once Cnaeus' wife and relatives had arranged a match in his absence, the senate allegedly voted to pay her dowry (cf. Ammianus Marcellinus XIIII.6.11 = Zonar. ix.3). Readers should take comfort from the fact that even Romans lost track of who was who.

16 Evans 1991: 29–31 has a number of Roman dowry stories of this type. See also Plutarch's *Life of Aristides 1, 1* and various entries in Valerius Maximus' chapter *de Paupertate (On Poverty) 4.4*.

17 Usually taken to be Ptolemy VIII, Euergetes II ('Physkon'), but see Gunther 1990 for a sceptical reading. She argues persuasively that the story was a plant, politically motivated.

18 See Horsfall 1989: xvii–xviii on his *exempla*. The fragments of letters allegedly by Cornelia to her son Gaius were found in one of the manuscripts of Nepos' work. The meaning and authenticity of these letters are discussed in Chapter 2.

19 Astin (1967: 2).

20 Polybius 31.23–30. A gentlemanly historian stranded by historical circumstance in Rome, Polybius was well placed to observe the Roman ruling group at close quarters during this interesting period and to explain Roman ways to fellow Greeks.

21 Many of Cato's speeches survived him and were known to later authors like Cicero, Nepos, Appian and Sallust. But see Fraccaro 1914: 15. Plutarch himself repeated many of Cato's famous sayings, thereby preserving them until now.

Astin has a long appendix (1967: 248–269) of Aemilianus' sayings, which were cited in the ancient world but are not as appealing to the modern taste as Cato's pithy aphorisms.

22 Polybius' account represents the process as a conscious one on Aemilianus' part. See Chapter 2.

23 Liv. 34.1. See Chapter 3 on the repeal of this wartime austerity measure, which limited the display of wealth by Roman women.

24 To distinguish him from his adoptive grandson (also termed 'Africanus' for crushing Carthage again in 146 BCE), to whom I refer throughout as Scipio Aemilianus or, more simply, Aemilianus.

25 Scullard 1951: 290–303 provides a helpful summary of the sources, issues and scholarly views concerning the so-called 'Scipio trials' involving Scipio Africanus the elder and his brother Lucius, but it is a very murky area and of little direct relevance to Cornelia. On Africanus generally, see Scullard 1970, esp. 18–32 on his legend.

26 The Romans (as we do) defined their history as pre- and post-Gracchi: Cic. *de Re pub.*1.31; Stockton 1979: 37.

27 These ups and downs continued in the century following the death of Tiberius Gracchus. Roman politics of the Late Republic 133–31 BCE was characterized by conflict between *populares*, who took legislation to the popular assembly via plebeian tribunes, and the *optimates*, who generally favoured traditional senatorial processes. This is a simplification. The two groups were not as clearly drawn as modern political parties. *Popularis* slogans and heroes were revived during the civil conflict of the 80s BCE and invoked by the historian Sallust (*c.*86–35 BCE) and, paradoxically, given some respectability by Julius Caesar's great-nephew Octavian/Augustus, who emerged from slaughter to found a monarchic dynasty which maintained some Republican forms. See Chapters 4 and 5, on the relatively favourable imperial treatment of the Gracchi. See also n. 34 below.

28 Bauman 1992: 48–49 and Petrocelli 1994: 60 both treat Sempronia seriously.

29 Moir (1983) has offered the ingenious suggestion that Pliny's expression *alternant* meant that she had six girls, then six boys. Her calculations of the considerable time which Cornelia's husband Tiberius spent abroad narrows the opportunities for her repeated impregnations.

30 Münzer 1900: 1592; Carcopino 1928: 70; Moir 1983: 143 have come to different conclusions about Cornelia's date of birth, but all suggestions are based on the same type of evidence, namely Plin. *HN* 7.57 and the birth dates of Tiberius (junior) and Gaius.

31 Tac. *Ann.* 4.34–5; Dio 57.24.4. Cremutius Cordus committed suicide 25 CE. His daughter was the Marcia to whom Seneca the younger addressed his consolation on the death of her son. He recalled her courage and determined filial piety in the face of her father's sufferings (*ad Marciam 1.1–5*). And see *PIR*: Marcia 395 (Dessau).

32 On Arria (elder and younger) and Fannia and their roles, see e.g. Plin. *Ep.*3.16, 7.19 and Sherwin-White's informative but strangely unsympathetic notes in his commentary *ad loc.*, esp. 1966: 424–426.

33 See Chapter 3 for more detail on the location and nature of the villas of Cornelia and of Sempronia's husband Aemilianus.

34 The Gracchan *popularis* cause survived Tiberius' assassination in 133 BCE, but was virtually driven underground for a time after Gaius' death in 121 BCE. The successful prosecution in 110 BCE of Opimius, the consul responsible for Gaius Gracchus' assassination, marks the beginning of the *popularis* resurgence. While not total, its success was considerable, culminating in the temporary alliance with Marius and the expulsion of Metellus Numidicus, but collapsing in 100 BCE

when, once more, its leaders (Saturninus, Glaucia and Equitius) were killed and vilified. On the *popularis/optimate* distinction, see n. 27 above.

2 People, politics, propaganda

1 Another simplification of issues I have covered exhaustively (or to my own exhaustion) in publications elsewhere. A woman could leave the family of her birth by transferring to the *manus* (lit. 'hand') of her husband on marriage or by becoming a Vestal. Aristocratic women in this century seem usually to have married by that form, which later became unusual. See esp. Dixon 1985c, 1992a: 61–97. A man could be adopted into another family, but, like Scipio Aemilianus, would continue to honour his biological parents and to benefit from the connections of his birth, as for example when Scipio Aemilianus and his brother accompanied their birth father to Pydna, in Macedon, after they had been adopted into other noble families.
2 It would also be interesting to know the origin of the antipathy between her sons and her elder sister's son, Publius Scipio Nasica, but I have narrowed my focus here to issues affecting the characterization of Cornelia herself.
3 A few of the many scholars who treat various aspects of this development include Badian 1972; Hopkins 1978; Harris 1985; Gruen 1990; Evans 1991.
4 Post-Second Punic war, that is (218–201 BCE). The Romans prosecuted wars throughout this century and the men of Cornelia's family were often abroad – in Spain, north Africa or Sardinia – in connection with them.
5 As always, we try to fix some dates from the few we know. Aemilius Paulus, biological father of Aemilianus, had given him and his brother over for adoption by the time he celebrated his triumph in 167 BCE. The death of his two younger sons at the time of this consummate honour provided ancient commentators with an irresistible example of the irony of fate (Polyb. 26.21.1.9; Diodorus 31.11; Plut. *Aem.P.* 35; cf. Cic. *Fam.* 4.6; Val.Max. 5.10.2). On the health of Aemilianus' adoptive father, Publius Cornelius Scipio, see Cic. *Brutus 77.* Aemilianus' distribution of his adoptive grandmother's estate on her death in 162 BCE implies that both his adoptive father (*RE 'Cornelius' 331*) and uncle (*RE 325*) had died by then (Polyb. 31.25–7) and see Walbank (1979, III: 503 *ad* 31.26.2).
6 The military practice continued. By Cicero's time, the nobility had become sufficiently cultured for some of their leading members to serve also as models of oratory or legal expertise – witness Cicero's association with Q. Mucius Scaevola ('the *augur*'). This system of mentorship was distinct from the more formal teaching which the elite continued to get from professionals who, as their social inferiors, filled a different role in patronal relations.
7 Plut. *TG* 21.7; Diod. 34/5.7.3; Astin 1967: 263–264.
8 Carcopino 1928: 85–127; Badian 1956: 220.
9 The main sources for the events of the two tribunates are Appian *BC 1.1–26* and Plutarch's *Lives* of *Tiberius* and *Gaius Gracchus*, esp. *TG 8–20, GG 4–18*. Plutarch (45–125 CE) lived a couple of centuries later but drew on earlier accounts. Appian, who came from Alexandria, lived in the second century BCE. Cicero's (106–43 BCE) and Sallust's (*c*.86–35 BCE) works, composed in the generations following the events, are scattered with references to the Gracchi. The brothers appeal eternally to students and the lay public but for some reason they do not attract as much scholarly attention these days from ancient historians as they used to. Any standard work on Roman Republican history will supply plenty of references for the avid reader to pursue. Be warned that works on 'the Gracchi' are mostly about Tiberius.
10 E.g. Astin 1967; Earl 1963; and Badian 1972.

11 E.g. Mitford 1954: 169. Cf. Dixon 1992b: 210–212.

12 For elaborations and examples, see Garlick *et al.* 1992.

13 Plut. *TG 8.6, 17.5–6*; Cic. *Brutus 104, de Amicitia 37*. Blossius of Cumae and Diophanes of Mitylene were both Stoics. Their impact on the political thinking of the Gracchi is debatable – and continues to *be* debated – Dudley 1941; Badian 1972: 678–681; Stockton 1979: 84–85; Becker 1964; Nicolet 1965, 1967: 148–163, 192–195. Blossius, a Campanian from Cumae, was a political follower of Tiberius. See Chapter 3 ('Culture wars') for speculation about Cornelia's philosophical interests.

14 Many great generals were to suffer such humiliations throughout the late Republican period. Denying or delaying the ratification of a treaty or the celebration of a triumph was one of those satisfyingly spiteful opportunities which senators revelled in visiting on their enemies – or just on fellow senators who had been a little too successful. In this case, the repudiation was even more humiliating – the treaty was deemed treasonably favourable to the enemy and the pro-consul Mancinus was ritually handed over to them (Plut. *TG 5–6*).

15 See esp. Hallett 1984; Dixon 1985c.

16 E.g. Sen. *ad Helviam 14.3.3.*

17 Appian *BC 1.9–11*; Cic. *pro Sestio 103*; Vel.Pat. 2.2.3; Plut. *TG 9–10.*

18 See e.g. Hopkins 1978: 15–25 *et passim*. These things vary with fashion. Badian's impressive 1972 survey is now a historical curiosity in its own right. It heralds the scepticism about claims that 'the whole of Italy' was depopulated by the agricultural changes and reflects the usual anglophone antagonism to contemporary Marxist analyses of the Gracchan reforms. The article also foreshadows the current interest in myth and image as political factors. See Evans 1991: 49 n.149 for a guide to proponents of the 'new' scepticism.

19 Astin 1967: 92–93; Badian 1972: 687, 691.

20 Cf. Phillips 1978; Dixon 1988: 215–232.

21 By interposing his veto against fellow tribune Tiberius in 133 BCE, Octavius had set in train the tragic events which led to Tiberius' death. See n. 46 below.

22 Or, perhaps, that they erected the statue and 'later' added the inscription. The reference to her sons in the plural ('the Gracchi') would have been more appropriate in any case after the death of both sons. See Chapter 4 ('The icon') for a more detailed discussion of the likelihood of when or if the statue was erected.

23 'Many of Gaius' references to her are recorded as being delivered against one of his opponents, in a rhetorical and public venue (*rhetorikos kai agoraios*)' (Plut. *GG 4*). Cf. Sen. *ad Helviam 16.6.* Stockton 1979: 217–225 has surviving fragments of Gaius' sayings and speeches with some commentary.

24 On the children of Tiberius and Gaius Gracchus, their likely sex, survival and dates of birth, see Astin 1967: 319–321; Stockton 1979: 30 and the discussion below.

25 Cic. *de Or. III.214 (= ORF 61).*

26 Cf. *ORF 65–66.*

27 Plutarch's formulaic 'They say' (*GG 13.2*) indicates an unnamed written source for some of these imputations. The passage concerning Cornelia's behaviour with guests at Misenum in her old age (*GG 19*) is longer and contains circumstantial detail. I think it likely that it originated with Sempronia or a loyal family dependent.

28 Plut. *GG 2*. But, as Badian rightly points out (1967: 162–167), such international prestige and connections did not necessarily translate to power at Rome, where they aroused *invidia*.

29 The *cursus honorum*, usually termed 'ladder' of office in English, refers to the conventional sequence of a senatorial career. The convention was progressively

strengthened by statute, most notably the *lex Villia annalis* of 180 BCE, to guard against the premature promotion of charismatic generals.

30 Cf. the remark made by Cato the elder (*Cat.mai. 15.3*) that prosecutions were a form of family piety. Ambitious politicians in the late Republic drew attention to their famous ancestors in public speeches, funeral ceremonies and, later, in coin issues, such as Brutus' reference in Caesar's heyday to his own eponymous ancestor's role in bringing down the monarchy in the sixth century BCE.

31 Although Aulus Gellius (2.13.1–2) interpreted the passage differently.

32 *ORF fr.47*, p. 190: 'nec quisquam de P. Africani et Tiberi Gracchi familia nisi ego et puer restaremus'. The term '*puer*' had numerous meanings, according to the context. It did not necessarily denote a very young boy and it could even (rarely) be used of a girl.

33 E.g. Münzer 1920: 270–273; Astin 1967: 319–321.

34 On the manuscript tradition, see Marshall (1977, 1983) and Hemelrijk (1999: 349). On the question of their possible role (or not) in Nepos' work, see Horsfall (1987, 1989).

35 *Legimus epistulas Corneliae matris Gracchorum: apparet filios non tam in gremio educatos quam in sermone matris.*

36 Cicero was born 106 BCE, at the time of the *popularis* revival. Atticus was a contemporary, Brutus somewhat younger. Scholars do not all agree that Cornelia's letters were published. The Latin plural 'we read' (*legimus*) can simply mean 'I read' so may refer here only to Cicero himself. Emily Hemelrijk (1999: 146–153, 349) observes – *pace* Instinsky 1971: 184–185 – that there was no meaningful distinction between Roman 'publication' and circulation among friends.

37 The headings to each segment are scribes' additions. The first is prefaced by 'Words from a letter of Cornelia [mother] of the Gracchi, excerpted from Cornelius Nepos' book on the Latin historians' (*verba ex epistula Corneliae Gracchorum ex libro Cornelii Nepotis de Latinis historicis excerpta*), the second simply *eadem alio loco* (the same author, in a different place).

38 See Instinsky (1971). As always, Hemelrijk (1999: 193–197, 349–352) provides an excellent guide to the issues.

39 I agree with Coarelli (1978: 26) that this period is more likely than the alternative period of active *popularis*/optimate propaganda, 87–82 BCE.

40 E.g. *insanire, miscenda atque perturbanda re publica, dementia* typical *optimate* language equating reform with political and mental disturbance. Political doublespeak is not a new invention.

41 *Gracchorum eloquentiae multum contulisse accepimus Corneliam matrem, cuius doctissimus sermo in posteros quoque est epistulis traditus.*

42 Hemelrijk (1999: 351 n. 49) argues that this silence can be explained away by the changing attitude to the Gracchi. But one could hardly accuse Cicero, a key element in the source tradition, of being adulatory. His oratorical tributes to the brothers are offset by political condemnation, e.g. *Brutus 103*. He would have had no reason to refrain from condemning Gaius' defiance of his mother if the letters he knew had indicated such a thing. Later sources also incorporate criticism of the Gracchi, e.g. Appian *BC 1.1–26*; Dio *frag. 83.15*. There are even traces of a tradition hostile to Cornelia herself – see below.

43 Plut. *GG 13.2*. The relevant passage begins with the 'They say' (*legousi*) formula.

44 See the references below to Gaius' speeches mentioning her (*ORF 197ff.*). Plutarch seems to reproduce traces of critical traditions (witness this accusation and the 'blame' which attached to Cornelia for firing her sons with excessive ambition, Plut. *TG 8.7*; cf. *GG 19*) and Appian's only reference to Cornelia is his transmission of the rumour that she and her daughter conspired to murder Scipio Aemilianus (*BC 1.20*).

45 Possibly explaining why her statue outlived the violent end of the *popularis* revival. Its continued existence in the porticus Metelli might have been the only lasting revenge of one great line (the Sempronii Gracchi), which dropped out of the consular lists for so long, on that other great plebeian noble family, the Caecilii Metelli, whose more enduring success in the fertility stakes had insured that their prominence would weather the ups and downs of late Republican politics.

46 M. Octavius, a fellow tribune of Tiberius Gracchus in 133 BCE, imposed his veto against Tiberius. Plut. *TG* 10.1; Dio *fr.* 83.4; Appian *BC* 1.12. See Astin 1967: 87, 346–347 on his motives and alignment.

47 Gaius' father had also been a *tribunus plebis*, a standard rung in the ladder of office for members of the plebeian nobility (like the Caecilii Metelli). Roman wives are sometimes represented as following Andromache's literary tradition of useless attempts at stopping their husbands from doing what a man has to do (Plutarch's examples include Gaius Gracchus' wife Licinia and Caesar's wife Calpurnia). But, even in famous instances of mother–son conflict, there is no hint of a mother from this social group wanting to prevent her son from pursuing a political career and winning fame. Cornelia seems a particularly unlikely example for the honour, *pace* Hemelrijk (1999: 351 n. 49).

48 Cf. Scipio Aemilianus' exploitation of his generosity to his birth mother as a calculated step in his political career (Polyb. 31.26.1–10).

49 The word 'later' – *hysteron* – is generally taken to apply to the erection of the statue, but it could as easily go with the verb 'inscribed'.

50 Hemelrijk (1999: 266–267 n. 46) dismisses the notion that this or any other statue of a woman was placed in such a public venue in Republican times. Cf. Coarelli 1978: 20–25; Chioffi 1999; Stegman 1997 and see the discussion in Chapter 4 ('The icon') of why Augustus might have installed or restored such a statue.

51 The crucial role of the Metelli in the rise of the 'new man' Marius and his breach from the grudging patronage of this great family is told with verve and partisanship by Sallust in his 'War with Jugurtha' (*BJ*) as well as by Plutarch in his *Life of Marius*. I am avoiding that particular diversion here, to concentrate on the Gracchan aspect of the propaganda wars.

52 These comments apply, whatever the character of the trial, its 'judges' and the charges. Cf. Cic. *Sest 101; Inscr. Ital. 13.3.16b* on the case and the issues. For Sempronia's role and the significance of the appearance of a woman of her standing at such a public event, see Herrmann 1964: 90–1 and the more authoritative Bauman 1992: 48–50, 231.

53 Cf. Val.Max. 9.7.2; *ORF (2) fr.47 (p. 190) = Schol.Bob. Sull p. 81 Stangl.*; Plut. *GG* 15.2. I do not necessarily endorse all the conclusions of Astin (1967: 319–321) but his discussion includes a very useful summary of the issues, scholarly views and sources concerning the likely dates of Tiberius Gracchus' marriage to Claudia and of the deaths of his children and those of Gaius. See also Stockton 1979: 30 n. 32; Earl 1963: 67–69.

3 Culture wars

1 The serious impact on Roman agriculture, manpower and therefore politics is touched on in the preceding chapter ('People, politics, propaganda') as it relates to Cornelia.

2 Periodization is seldom clear-cut. Authors such as Ennius (*c.*239–169BCE), and Plautus (250–184) straddled the century mark. Elite authors of prose works (e.g. Cato, Fannius, Rutilius Rufus and Gaius Gracchus himself) are important sources for this period, although in many cases we have only echoes and fragmentary quotes passed on by much later writers. See Chapter 1 ('Fact and Fable').

3 Liv. 38.52.1; Cic. *Off. 3.2*. See d'Arms 1970: 15–16.
4 Hemelrijk 1999: 24 and *passim*, especially chapter 2.
5 Horsfall 1989: 54. Cato learned Greek later in life – Plut. *Cat.mai.2.4*; Cornelius Nepos' *Life* 3.1–2. Horsfall's commentary and discussion (1989 *passim*) on the Cato fragments is much more informative and intelligent than Nepos'. Cf. Dench 1996 on Cato's model of Sabine purity.
6 Cato's vehemence in pursuit of political opponents was so great (Plut. *Cat.mai. 15*; Liv. 38.50ff.) that some might think it was personal. He clearly threw himself into such stoushes with gusto and even other Romans were impressed that he was still conducting vindictive lawsuits in his eighties, but he acquired his enemies (in the usual fashion of factional politics anywhere, anytime) in a job lot when he aligned himself with his patrons Fabius Maximus and Valerius Flaccus (Plut. *Cat.mai. 3*).
7 Consider the words which Livy (who knew Cato's speeches) puts into Cato's mouth at 34.4. See below on the debate about the repeal during Cato's consulship 195 BCE of the *lex Oppia*, passed in 215 BCE as a wartime austerity measure limiting women's use of gold and purple and their access to carriages. Plutarch speaks naively of Cato's misgivings about Scipionic extravagance and its corrupting effects on the soldiery as being aroused during his service under Africanus in 204 BCE, but this reference is likely to have been taken from a speech much later in Cato's career. In 204, Cato was a promising and ambitious new player from outside the hereditary ruling group, eager to prove his mettle to a powerful patron by attacking his enemy. That was business, not personal, as the players in the 'Godfather' movies would say. The moral indignation against Scipio may well be a retrospective rationale, trumpeted by an older and more established Cato. Cato would have been deeply embittered when Scipio ousted him from his consular command in Spain some ten years later. Plutarch's account of the incident a decade later (*Cat.mai. 11*), presumably based on Cato's own written version, naturally presents Cato in a favourable light but cannot obscure the central fact that the aristocrat Scipio deprived the 'new man' Cato of an opportunity for distinction. Business again.
8 E.g. the Bacchic persecutions of 186 BCE, the prohibition 185 BCE of a permanent theatre, the expulsion of two Epicurean philosophers in 173 and of more philosophers and rhetoricians in 161 BCE, sumptuary legislation such as the *lex Orchia* and the *lex Fannia*; cf. the *lex Voconia* of 169 BCE and the repeal 195 BCE of the *lex Oppia* (see preceding note).
9 Coarelli 1978: 18–20 (the arts in the Augustan era) and Hemelrijk 1999: 93–95 (literature) provide examples of this well-known phenomenon.
10 Liv. 38.51.1. See Moscovich 1988: 109.
11 E.g. Polyb. 31.23–30. Cf. Cic. *Rep. 1.14ff.* (culture), Plin. *NH 33.14.1* (integrity and restraint). And see Astin 1967: 342.
12 Polyb. 18.35; Liv. *per. 46.1*; Plut. *Aem.P. 39.5*.
13 *Pace* modern depictions, the impropriety was as likely to be unsuitable Greek-style dress or dancing at dinner parties, as sexual misbehaviour. Cicero's prosecution speeches against Piso and Verres give a good sample, e.g. II *Verr.* 1.34, 5.80–3.
14 One of the many signs that Cato's *Lex Oppia* speech was penned by Livy is the reference to his 'well-known' (Liv. 34.4) concerns about women's extravagance, probably an anachronistic reference to his 169 BCE speech in favour of the *lex Voconia*, which *would* have been well known to Livy's readers (cf. Aul.Gell. 17.6). And see Badian 1956: 220; Horsfall 1987: 233, 1989: 41 on the attitude of historians in the ancient world to quotation.
15 Boyer 1950; Gardner 1986: 170–177; Dixon 1985b.
16 Peppe 1984: 60–69; Dixon 1988: 41–70.

17 This famous story is told with little variation by Polybius 31.22.1–4 and Diodorus 31.26.1–2; 27.1. Cf. Liv. *per. 46*; Plut. *Aem.P. 39.8–10*; Val.Max. 4.4.9. I remind readers that such dowry stories attach to famous men, to illustrate virtue and paradox, cf. Varro *RR 3.16.2* on Appius Claudius, Plin. *NH 34.36* on Mummius, the examples listed by Evans 1991: 54–55 and the stories we reviewed in Chapter 1 on Scipio Africanus and his daughters' dowries.

18 Polyb. 31.23–30. Possibly, two successive five-year plans: once he had established his magnanimity (*megalopsychia*) and integrity (*katharotes*), Aemilianus set to work on the next stage, to gain a reputation for bravery (*andreia*) – Polyb. 31.25.9; cf. 31.30.1–4. In 1979, Walbank (III. 502) needed to rationalize this oddity. I, too, was bemused by the notion in the 1980s, but I am accustomed in the twenty-first century to hearing schoolchildren comparing life plans and goals on the bus. Aemilianus would seem normal to them.

19 Best read together with Walbank's incomparable commentary 1979: III. 499– 514. Cf. Boyer 1950; Dixon 1985a. Diodorus' parallel account (31.27–8) adds little.

20 That is since her divorce from Aemilius Paulus some time before 181 BCE (Plut. *Aem.P. 35.1*). The approximate date of Paulus' second marriage can be reckoned by counting back from the reported ages of the sons of that union (14 and 12) at the time of their premature deaths in 167 BCE, the year of Aemilius Paulus' triumph (Plut. *Aem.P. 34*). He must have remarried *c.*181 at the latest (Plut. *Aem.P. 35.1*).

21 Polyb. 31.26.10. Livy's account of the sequence of the women's demonstration of 195 to ensure the repeal of the *lex Oppia* makes it clear that women did have an effective network, extending into 'the country' (Liv. 34.8), presumably the basis for the organization of these religious occasions. Consider the historic examples cited by the tribune L. Valerius (34. 5) of mass female gestures in time of state emergency – Peppe 1984: 46–50, 80–91. On Papiria's death, Aemilianus then passed the whole set on to his sisters, not to Aemilia's daughters, the two Corneliae – Polyb. 31.28.7–9; Diodorus 31.27.7.

22 *Pace* Polyb. 31.28.3; Plut. *Aem.P. 39.5*, etc. the myth of Aemilius Paulus' 'poverty' is belied by other indications of the size of his estate – cf. Frank *ESAR I*, 208–209.

23 As Plutarch says elsewhere in the *Life* (19.5), Cato made many boasts about his superior moral and physical regimen. Plut. *Cat.mai. 4.4–6* was probably based on his speech *de sumptu suo* which Aulus Gellius cites 13.24.1–2. Cf. Dench 1996.

24 Her sons, Lucius (no. 325 = Henze, *RE IV.1431–3*) and Aemilianus' adoptive father Publius (no. 331 = Münzer, *RE IV.1437–8*), must have died in the meantime. There were various means of ensuring female succession. Instituting Aemilianus heir and assigning the two daughters a *legatum partitionis* would have given them an equal share in the estate but obliged Aemilianus to distribute it. Very likely the two Corneliae were *in manu mariti* so that their husbands technically took the share and administered it until their deaths, when it was paid out (classified as dowry – Cic. *Top. 23*) like the dowry to Aemilius Paulus' second wife (see above) from the joint family estate.

25 Boyer 1950; Dixon 1985a.

26 Val.Max. 2.8; Hopkins 1978: 24–27.

27 Scipio Africanus the elder: Liv. 28.38, 45; Appian *Hisp. 38*; Polyb. 11.33.7 (205 BCE), 31.49 (200 BCE). T. Quinctius Flamininus: Liv. 34.52 (lasting three days). L. Aemilius Paulus: Plut. *Aem.P. 32–34*. And see Moscovich 1988 on Scipio's 205 BCE possibly unofficial 'triumph'.

28 Evans (1991: 59) lists some of the more spectacular funerals and the associated games and public dinners in this period of agonistic ostentation which inspired sumptuary laws like the *lex Orchia* of 181 BCE and the *lex Fannia* of 161 BCE.

29 Other sources, e.g. Aul.Gell. 6.14.8–10, add Critolaus the Peripatetic to this list. Gellius refers to comments by P. Rutilius Rufus and Polybius about the different rhetorical styles employed by the heads of the three schools – cf. Cic. *Brutus* 117–9.

30 Cicero checked the date with Atticus (*Att.* 12.23.2) for use in his own writings, e.g. *Acad.* 2.13.7. And cf. Plin. *NH.*7.112; Cornelius Nepos *Cato 32*; and Horsfall 1989: 54 *ad loc.*

31 Cato allegedly learned Greek late in life (Plut. *Cat.mai. 2.5* – from the poet Ennius, according to *Vir.Illust. 47.1*), but given his age at this time (79 or so), he must have taken the plunge by then. Consider his interpolation in the senate (*Cat.mai. 22.7*). At Pydna in 168 BCE, the victorious Aemilius Paulus allegedly addressed the defeated Macedonian King Perseus in Greek and his own *consilium* in Latin (Polyb. 29.20.1–4; Liv. 45.8.6–7; and Walbank 1979: III. 392.

32 Selective expulsions from Rome took place from time to time, e.g. in 173 and 161 BCE. See Gruen 1990: 158–192, esp. 171–175 for an account of these reactions in their general political context, including sumptuary legislation and intermittent religious intolerance.

33 Cicero produced Romanized versions of select Stoic principles, e.g. in his *de Officiis*, much of it based on Panaetius. Imperial Stoics whose writings survive include Musonius Rufus (fragmentary), various works (*Epistulae Morales*) by Seneca the younger and the jottings ('*To himself*') of the emperor Marcus ('Aurelius'), usually termed *Meditations*.

34 Tac. *Agricola 4.4*; Suet. *Nero 52*; SHA (Iul.Capit) *Marc. Ant. 6.9*.

35 Cic. *Brutus 79*.

36 E.g. Becker 1964; Stockton 1979: 38. Badian 1972: 679–680 is understandably critical of Becker and more impressed by Nicolet's suggestions (1965 esp. 149–153) that Tiberius was probably influenced by Spartan models of land equalization. See also Nicolet 1967.

37 Plut. *GG 19.4*. In time, the philosophic approach to suffering was integrated in ideal Roman elite behaviour and was routinely invoked in letters of condolence (Horsfall 1989: 89). Its incorporation in stock descriptions of those who bore suffering in an admirable way makes it difficult for us to distinguish the strictly philosophical from the social norm.

38 12.3, *On the Constancy of the Wise Man* (*To Serena, That the Wise Man cannot suffer damage or injury*). And compare the views of second-century heads of the Stoic school in vol. III of the Stoic Fragments (*SVF*). See esp. *SVF III. pp.* 210–213 for the views of Diogenes the Babylonian (one of the envoys who caused such a sensation in Rome in 155 BCE) on courage (*andreia*) and Cic. *Tusc.Disp.* 3.83, 4.24 *et passim*.

39 Cf. Dixon 2001: 89–90; Rawson (1976).

40 Cicero was indignant when accused of frequenting Baiae – the mere word by then was a synonym for *la dolce vita* (d'Arms 1970: 52–55). He exploited that association in his attack on Clodia in his *pro Caelio 35* but elsewhere he associates villas with cultural activity (e.g. Cic. *Off. 3.2* on Scipio Africanus; *Fam. 9.4* on Varro's Casinum villa) or innocent recreation – *de Or. 2.22*. The Campanian coast continued in the imperial period to be a favourite haunt of the literati (d'Arms 1970: 140–149).

41 Plut. *GG 19.1*; Orosius 5.12.9. For differing conclusions, see Carcopino 1928: 105–106; d'Arms 1970: 22; Petrocelli 1994: 55.

42 Cf. the story of Scipio Africanus preparing to fend off the pirates who approached his well-fortified villa (see below), only to learn that they were tourists who wanted to admire his celebrity (Val.Max. 2.10.2). The ever-popular Kentucky Fried Rat story has always *happened* to a friend/relative of a friend of the person who tells it. Wherever I went on lecture tours to US universities in the

1980s, I was treated to the local variant of a *topos* about a certain very distinctive ancient historian and assured that the mistaken identity/recognition error (worthy of New Comedy) had *really* happened (though never to the storyteller) when he had arrived at that particular place to give a guest lecture.

43 Plut. *TG.* 8.6; Val.Max. 4.7.1 on Blossius' bad influence and his interrogation by Laelius; cf. Cic. *Brut.* 104, *de Amicitia* 37; on Laelius' connections with Campania, see Dudley 1941. Cf d'Arms 1970: 292, 317 on Blossius' family at Puteoli.

44 Plut. *TG* 20.4–7; Dudley 1941: 98–99. In an appealing variant on the usual philosopher-king association, Blossius joined the revolt of Aristonicus and committed suicide when it was ultimately defeated. For a time, it was a strong movement, including former slaves and peasants who mobilized to fight the Romans and their oppressive lackeys in the Greek East. See Martinez Lacy (1995) for other popular revolts.

45 Cato, *fr.*185, p. 75 *ORF* ² (Festus p. 282,4); *villae expolitissimae* – Scipio Aemilianus *fr.*20, p. 129 *ORF* ² S= Aulus Gellius 2.20.6.

46 Seneca is not reliable on such fine points. His historical sense is often confused and he makes many avoidable, elementary mistakes – more than is reasonable. Anybody can, of course, slip up, but in general Seneca compares poorly with Cicero's standards of checking historical dates and personalities with Atticus – see the examples cited by Horsfall 1989: 96. Cf. Plin. *Ep.* 6.16 and 20 to Tacitus.

47 Cf. *Vita Terentii* 3 = Nepos frag. 54, *Vir.Illust.* for the story of Laelius writing in his villa – Horsfall 1989: 119. Cicero's dialogues provide a number of references, ultimately emanating from Laelius himself. Other references to Aemilianus' villa at Lavernium and Laelius' property in or near Puteoli have been collected by D'Arms 1970: 19–21, e.g. Macrobius *Sat. 3.164* (based on a Cicero fragment).

48 Hemelrijk 1999: 53 and nn. pp. 256–258 (citing Vitruvius *Arch. 1.2.7; 6.4.1*); Casson 2001: 69–71. Thanks as usual to Cicero, we have more detailed accounts for the later period, e.g. Cic. *Fin. 3.2.7–9* and his letters to Atticus; cf. Plin. *Ep. 2.17.8*.

49 Cf. Hemelrijk 1999: 54, for the suggestion that Cornelia might have enjoyed access to the library of Aemilius Paulus (cf. Plut. *Aem.P. 6.5, 28.6*). She speculates p. 257 n. 167 about whether Sempronia inherited the library of her husband Scipio Aemilianus on his death in 129 BCE. Her discussion of Roman libraries and women's access to them (pp. 53–57) is an excellent review of the subject. Cf. Casson 2001.

50 Menelaus of Marathus (Phoenicia) is mentioned by Cicero in association with Gaius Gracchus (*Brutus* 100) in the exchange between Gaius and Fannius, whose speech was believed to have been written by the *grammaticus* (*homo litteratus*) Persius.

4 The icon

1 Dixon 1991: 108, 111–112; and see Hänninen (forthcoming) on Cornelia in exemplary lists. I am grateful to Dr Lena Larsson for drawing this paper to my attention.

2 E.g. Plut. *TG 1.4–6*; Cic. *de Div. I.36, II.62*; Plin. *NH 7.122*.

3 *Con.Praec. 145 E*, where she is referred to as 'Cornelia of Scipio'.

4 Plut. *TG 1.3*; Gunther 1990.

5 E.g. Aurelia mother of Caesar; Atia, mother of Octavian/Augustus. See Tac. *Dialogus 28* and the lists below.

6 Lightman and Zeisel 1977; Dixon 1992a: 39, 123, 212.

7 Of course, there were other orators who distinguished themselves before the Gracchi, and Cicero lists them e.g. *Brutus 78ff.*

8 Badian 1972: 687, 691 n. 63 thinks he continued to be pro-Gracchan. His behaviour even in 133 BCE, as the consul resident in Rome during Tiberius' tribunate, is difficult to read. On the Mucii Scaevolae, see Münzer's family tree, cols. 413–4, *RE.VII*. On Laelia, see Cic. *Brutus 211, de Oratore 3.45*.

9 Using 190 as Cornelia's date of birth, 175 as her date of marriage. See again Chapter 1 and Moir (1983) for the issues.

10 E.g. Cic. *Fam. 5.16*, and consider Pliny's comments *Ep. 5.16*. Cf. Seneca's impatience with excessive or superficial (i.e. un-philosophical) modes of dealing with grief – *Ep.Mor. 9.9.1, ad Helviam 17.1–3*.

11 OPVS TISICRATIS/CORNELIA AFRICANI F/GRACCHORVM.

12 And see Chapter 2 above, on the political context. Coarelli (1978: 15ff.) also argues, even more controversially, that the statue base found on the spot in the late nineteenth century was the original.

13 The porticus of Metellus was established some time between 146–131 BCE (Dio 44.43). Cf. Coarelli 1978: 15.

14 Plin. *NH 35.114, 139*. See Lewis 1988: 200.The building also housed two libraries (Greek and Latin), and a large chamber suitable even for senate meetings – Richardson 1992: 317–318 and figs. 70, 71.

15 See now Zanker 1988; Kleiner 1978; Wood 1999; Woodcock 1999.

16 This unusual use of the unadorned genitive *Gracchorum* to mean 'mother of the Gracchi', normally used after a woman's name to mean 'daughter of' or 'wife of', has bothered many scholars. Kajava (1989: 130) is reluctant to posit a gallery without independent evidence because the plural makes it clear that it refers in that expression to her sons, not to her husband (which would be '*Gracchi*', in the singular) and sees no need to posit a gallery.

17 Suet. *Aug. 34*; Dio 56.1–10. See Dixon 1988: 71–103.

18 The senate decreed the Altar in 13 BCE to show its appreciation of Augustus' successful 'pacification' programme, but the monument, which included Augustus' regal 'achievements' (*Res Gestae*), is generally treated as an integral part of Augustan propaganda. Its ingenious retrieval and restoration in the 1930s (MacKendrick 1960: 201–206) was part of a similar programme.

19 To seal a political pact with Antonius which, like the marriage, soon disintegrated, but not before Octavia had children with him. Octavia's role as wronged wife was established by her highly publicized trip to Tarentum ostensibly to effect a conjugal and political reconciliation – Plut. *M.Ant. 53*; Dio 49.33.3–4. See Bauman 1992: 96–97; Woodcock 1999: 103.

20 E.g. *RG* 1 and *passim*.

5 Afterlife

1 Contrast Seneca's regret (*ad Helviam 17.3–5*) that his father's conservatism had deprived his mother of the benefit of philosophy with *ad Helviam 16.6–7*, and *ad Marciam 16.1–4*, where Cornelia's exemplary dignity in bereavement is classed with that of other admirable Roman women, none of them particularly associated with philosophy.

2 Agrippina the younger, daughter of the Julio-Claudian prince Germanicus, secured Seneca's aid in teaching her son, who took the name of his imperial stepfather/great-uncle Claudius and, on the emperor's death in 54 CE, succeeded him as 'Nero', although Claudius had a son of his own. Seneca's influence on Nero ultimately outlasted his mother's but he, too, was eventually expelled from court and finally forced into suicide for suspected sedition – Tac. *Ann. 15. 63*. Agrippina's ambition is the point of the story that she had Nero's fortune told when he was a baby and was delighted at the prediction that he would be emperor, and only temporarily put off by the prediction that he would kill his

mother – yet another *topos* too good to keep to oneself – Suet. *Nero 6* (with the mandatory snake story for good value). Perhaps our understanding of Julio-Claudian palace politics would be different if we still had Agrippina's autobiography -Tac. *Ann. 4.53.3*; Hemelrijk 1999: 186–188.

3 See the preceding chapter ('The icon') on Augustus' assumption of lifelong tribunician power and the significance of the Ara Pacis Augustae and other propaganda projects.

4 Aelian *HV14.45*; Jerome (Hieronymus) *In Iovinianum 1.49 (320)C*; *Ep. 54.4: Cornelia vestra, pudicitiae simul et fecunditatis exemplar, Gracchos suos se genuisse laetata est?*

5 Dio 66.24 and see Coarelli 1978: 20; Hemelrijk 1999: 266.

6 See Fantham *et al.* 1994: 265 and the illustration, fig. 9.1, p. 266. Cf. Coarelli 1978: 20–21; Kajava 1989: 127; Petrocelli 1994: 64 and *contra*, Hemelrijk 1999: 267.

7 Fraser (2001: 437–438) cites a subtle visual reference by painter Mme Vignée Le Brun to Cornelia's jewels in a 1787 portrait of Queen Marie-Antoinette which stressed her role as 'Mother of the Children of France'.

8 The themes must pre-date Shakespeare, 'it being the intention that the windows, when all complete, shall unite harmoniously into one great theme'. 'Cornelia, Mother of the Gracchi' is window no. 2. All the windows were installed between 1879–1902 and can be viewed at http://www/college.harvard.edu/%7Ememhall/staingls.html

Bibliography

Abbreviations of standard works

ANRW   Temporini, H. (ed.) *Aufstieg und Niedergang der Römischen Welt*, (esp. vol. 1, *Von den Anfängen Roms bis zum Ausgang der Republik*, published 1972). Berlin, New York: de Gruyter.

ESAR1   Frank, T. (ed.) (1933) *An Economic Survey of Ancient Rome*, vol. 1, *Rome and Italy of the Republic*, Baltimore, MD: Johns Hopkins Press.

Fantham *et al.*   Fantham, E., Foley, H.P., Kampen, N.B., Pomeroy, S.B. and Shapiro, H.A. (1994) *Women in the Classical World. Image and Text*, New York, Oxford: Oxford University Press.

HRR   Peter, H. (ed.) (1967) *Historicorum Romanorum Reliquiae*, Stuttgart: Teubner.

LTUR   Steinby, E.M. (ed.) (1999) *Lexicon Topographicum Urbis Romae*, Rome: Quasar.

ORF   *Oratorum Romanorum Fragmenta Liberae Rei Publicae*, (fourth edition reproduced photographically 1975 from H. Malcovati (ed.) second edition 1953), Turin: Paravia.

PIR   *Prosopographia Imperii Romani*.

RE   (also referred to as 'Pauly-Wissowa') Wissowa, G. (new edition 1900) Paulys *Real-Encyclopädie der Classischen Altertumswissenschaft*, Stuttgart: Metzler.

Journal titles are given in full in the references below.

Works consulted

Astin, A.E. (1967) *Scipio Aemilianus*, Oxford: Clarendon.

Badian, E. (1956) Review of H. Malcovati, *Oratorum Romanorum Fragmenta Liberae Rei Publicae (Iteratis Curis Recensuit Collegit)*, *Journal of Roman Studies*, 46: 218–221.

—— (1958) *Foreign Clientelae*, Oxford: Clarendon.

—— (1972) 'Tiberius Gracchus and the Beginning of the Roman Revolution', in H. Temporini (ed.) *Aufstieg und Niedergang der Römischen Welt (ANRW)*, vol. 1: 668–731, Berlin, New York: de Gruyter.

Barnard, S. (1990) 'Cornelia and the Women of her Family', *Latomus*, 49: 383–392.

Bauman, R. (1992) *Women and Politics in Ancient Rome*, London: Routledge.

Becker, J.B. (1964) 'The influence of Roman Stoicism upon the Gracchi economic land reforms', *Parola del Passato*, 19: 125–134.

Bell, S.G. and Yalom, M. (1990) 'Introduction', in S.G. Bell and M. Yalom (eds) *Revealing Lives: Autobiography, Biography and Gender*, pp. 1–15, New York: SUNY Press.

Bernstein, A.E. (1978) *Tiberius Sempronius Gracchus: Tradition and Apostasy* (esp. pp. 42ff.), Ithaca, NY: Cornell University Press.

Blok, J. and Mason, P. (eds) (1987) *Sexual Asymmetry: Studies in Ancient Society*, Amsterdam: Gieben.

Boyer, G. (1950) 'Le droit successoral romain dans les oeuvres de Polybe', *Revue Internationale du Droit de l'Antiquité*, 4: 169–187.

Brodersen, K. (2000) 'Tiberius und Gaius Sempronius Gracchus – und Cornelia: die *res publica* zwischen Aristokratie, Demokratie und Tyrannis', in K-J. Hölkeskamp and E. Hölkeskamp (eds) *Von Romulus zu Augustus. Grosse Gestalten der römischen Republik*, pp. 172–186, München: Beck.

Carcopino, J. (1928) *Autour des Gracques. Études critiques*, Paris: Guillaume Budé (rep. 1967, Société d'Édition *Les Belles Lettres*).

Carro, D. (1993–1995) *Storia della Marina di Roma. Testimonianze dell' 'Antichità* (esp. no. 11 (1993 – Scipio Africanus and the war with Hannibal); 10 (1995 – Naval Consolidation and Scipio Aemilianus)), Rome: Rivista marittima, *Classica/ Le Cose della Flotta*.

Casson, L. (2001) *Libraries in the Ancient World*, New Haven, CT: Yale University Press; reprinted as a Yale Nota Bene paperback 2002.

Chioffi, L. (1999) 'Statua: Cornelia', in M. Steinby (ed.) *Lexicon Topographicum Urbis Romae*, pp. 357–359, Rome: Edizioni Quasar di Seveno Tognon.

Coarelli, F. (1978) 'La statue de Cornélie, Mère des Gracques et la crise politique à Rome au temps de Saturninus', in H. Zehnacker (ed.) *Le dernier siècle de la République romaine et l'époque augustéenne*, pp. 13–28, Strasbourg: AECR.

Cugusi, P. (1983) *Evoluzione e forme dell'epistolografia Latina nella tarda repubblica e nei primi due secoli dell'impero*, Rome: Herder.

d'Arms, J. (1970) *Romans on the Bay of Naples: A Social and Cultural Study of the Villas and their Owners from 150 BC to 400 AD*, Cambridge MA: Harvard University Press; reprinted F. Zevi (ed.) (2003): 15–225.

—— (1977) 'Proprietari e ville nel golfo di Napoli', *Atti dei Convegni Lincei*, 33: 347–363 (*I Campi Flegrei nell'archaeologia e nella storia*), Rome: Accademia nazionale dei Lincei; reprinted F. Zevi (ed.) (2003): 331–350.

—— (1979) 'Ville rustiche e ville di *otium*', in F. Zevi (ed.) *Pompeii 79, Raccolta di studi per il decimonono centenario dell'eruzione vesuviana*, pp. 65–86, Naples; reprinted F. Zevi (ed.) (2003): 351–383.

Dench, E. (1996) 'Images of Roman Austerity from Cato to Tacitus', in M. Cébeillac-Gervasoni (ed.) *Les élites municipales de l'Italie péninsulaire des Gracques à Néron*, pp. 247–254; Actes de la table ronde de Clermont-Ferrand, 28–30 Nov., 1991.

Dixon, S. (1984) '*Infirmitas Sexus*: Womanly Weakness in Roman Law', *Tijdschrift voor Rechtsgeschedenis/Legal History Journal*, 52: 343–371 (condensed version reprinted S. Dixon (2001): ch. 6).

—— (1985a) 'Polybius on Roman Women and Property', *American Journal of Philology*, 106: 147–170.

—— (1985b) 'Breaking the Law to Do the Right Thing: The Voconian Law in Ancient Rome', *Adelaide Law Review*, 9: 519–534.

—— (1985c) 'The Marriage Alliance in the Roman Elite', *Journal of Family History*, 10: 353–378.

—— (1988) *The Roman Mother*, London: Croom Helm.

—— (1991) 'The Sentimental Ideal of the Roman Family', in B. Rawson (ed.) *Marriage, Divorce and Children in Ancient Rome*, pp. 99–113, Oxford: Oxford University Press.

—— (1992a) *The Roman Family*, Baltimore, MD: Johns Hopkins University Press.

—— (1992b) 'The Enduring Theme: Domineering Dowagers and Scheming Concubines', in B. Garlick, S. Dixon and P. Allen (eds) *Stereotypes of Women in Power*, pp. 209–225, New York: Greenwood.

—— (2001) *Reading Roman Women: Sources, Genres and Real Life*, London: Duckworth.

Dudley, D.R. (1941) 'Blossius of Cumae', *Journal of Roman Studies*, 31: 94–99.

Duncan, C. (1973) 'Happy Mothers and Other New Ideas in French Art', *Art Bulletin*, 55: 570–583.

Earl, D. (1963) *Tiberius Gracchus: A Study in Politics*, Brussels: Berchem (Collection Latomus 66).

Evans, J.K. (1991) *War, Women and Children in Ancient Rome*, London: Routledge.

Fantham, E., Foley, H.P., Kampen, N.B., Pomeroy, S.B. and Shapiro, H.A. (1994) (= Fantham *et al.*), *Women in the Classical World. Image and Text*, New York, Oxford: Oxford University Press.

Ferrier, C.C. (1999) *Jean Devanny, Romantic Revolutionary*, Melbourne: Melbourne University Press.

Fraccaro, P. (1914) *Studi sull'età dei Gracchi: la tradizione storica sulla rivoluzione graccana*, Città di Castello; reprinted (1967), Rome: «l'erma» di Bretschneider (Studia Historica 41).

Frank, T. (ed.) (1933) *An Economic Survey of Ancient Rome*, Baltimore, MD: Johns Hopkins Press.

Fraschetti, A. (ed.) (1994) *Roma al Femminile*, Bari: Laterza.

Fraser, Lady A. (2001) *Marie-Antoinette: The Journey*, London: Doubleday.

Gardner, J.F. (1986) *Women in Roman Law and Society*, London: Croom Helm.

Garlick, B., Dixon, S. and Allen, P. (eds) (1992) *Stereotypes of Women in Power. Historical Perspectives and Revisionist Views*, New York: Greenwood.

Gruen, E. (1990) *Studies in Greek Culture and Roman Policy*, Leiden: Brill.

Gunther, L.M. (1990) 'Cornelia und Ptolemaios VIII. Zur Historizität des Heiratsantrages (Plut TG 1,3)', *Historia*, 39: 124–128.

Hallett, J.P. (1984) *Fathers and Daughters in Roman Society: Women and the Elite Family*, Princeton, NJ: Princeton University Press.

Hänninen, M.-L. (2007) '"How to be a Great Roman Lady", Images of Cornelia in Ancient Literary Tradition', in L. Larsson Lovén and A. Strömberg (eds) *Public Roles – Personal Status. Men and Women in Antiquity*. Proceedings of the third Nordic symposium on gender and women's history in Antiquity, Copenhagen, October 2003. Sävedalen: Paul Åström Press, forthcoming.

Harris, W. (1985) *War and Imperialism in Republican Rome 327–70 BC*, Oxford: Clarendon.

Hemelrijk, E. (1987) 'Women's Demonstrations in Republican Rome', in J. Blok and P. Mason (eds) *Sexual Asymmetry*, pp. 217–240, Amsterdam: Gieben..

—— (1999) *Matrona Docta*, London: Routledge.

Herrmann, C. (1964) *Le Rôle judiciaire et politique des femmes sous la République romaine*, Brussels: Latomus (Collection Latomus 67).

Hopkins, K. (1978) *Conquerors and Slaves*, Cambridge: Cambridge University Press.

Horsfall, N. (1987) 'The "Letter of Cornelia": Yet More Problems', *Athenaeum*, 65 n.s. Fasc I–II: 231–234.

—— (1989) *Cornelius Nepos. A Selection, including the Lives of Cato and Atticus*, Oxford: Clarendon Ancient History Series.

Huggins, R. and Huggins, J. (1994) *Auntie Rita*, Canberra: Aboriginal Studies Press.

Instinsky, H.U. (1971) 'Zur Echtheitsfrage der Brieffragmente der Cornelia Mutter der Gracchen', *Chiron*, 1: 177–189.

Kajava, M. (1989) 'Cornelia Africani f. Gracchorum', *Arctos*, 23: 119–131.

Kleiner, D.E. (1978) 'The Great Friezes of the Ara Pacis Augustae: Greek Sources, Roman Derivatives and Augustan Social Policy', *Mélanges de l'École Française de Rome: Antiquité*, 90: 753–785.

Konrad, C.F. (1989) 'Livy on the Betrothal of Cornelia Gracchi (38.57.7)', *Philologus*, 133: 155–157.

Lewis, R.G. (1988) 'Some Mothers', *Athenaeum*, n.s. 66: 198–200.

Lightman, M. and Zeisel, W. (1977) '*Univira*: An Example of Continuity and Change in Roman Society', *Church History*, 46: 19–32.

MacKendrick, P. (1960) *The Mute Stones Speak. The Story of Archaeology in Italy*, (1983 edition), New York: Norton.

Marr, D. (1996) 'Only What's Private Matters', paper delivered at the Australian National Library seminar Private Lives Revealed: Letters, Diaries, History, March. Online. Available HTTP: http://www.nla.gov.au/events/private/marr.html#one

Marshall, P.K. (1977) *The Manuscript Tradition of Cornelius Nepos*, Bulletin (BICS) supp. 37, Institute of Classical Studies, University of London.

—— (1983) 'Cornelius Nepos', in L.D. Reynolds (ed.) *Texts and Transmission. A Survey of the Latin Classics*, Oxford: Clarendon, pp. 247–248.

Martinez Lacy, R. (1995) *Rebeliones populares en la Grecia helenistica*, Mexico: Universidad nacional autónoma de México (Cuadernos del Centro de Estudios Clasicos 38).

Mitford, N. (1954) *Madame de Pompadour* (reprinted 1970 from 1968 revised edition), London: Sphere.

Moir, K.M. (1983) 'Pliny *HN* VII.57 and the Marriage of Tiberius Gracchus', *Classical Quarterly*, 33.1: 136–145.

Moscovich, M.J. (1988) 'Dio Cassius on Scipio's Return from Spain in 205 BC', *Ancient History Bulletin*, 2.5: 107–110.

Münzer, F. (1900) 'Cornelia', *RE IV*. cols 1592–5 (in addition to many other articles in the Paulys *Real-Encyclopädie* = *RE* on the 'Cornelii', 'Mucii Scaevolae' and 'Sempronii Gracchi' cited *ad loc.*).

—— (1920) *Römische Adelsparteien und Adelsfamilien*, Stuttgart: Metzler (1963 reprint of original).

Nicolet, C. (ed.) (1965) 'L'Inspiration de Tibérius Gracchus', *Revue des études anciennes*, 18: 142–158.

—— (ed.) (1967) *Les Gracques ou Crise agraire et Révolution à Rome*, Paris: Julliard (Collection Archives).

Peppe, L. (1984) *Posizione giuridica e ruolo sociale della Donna romana in età repubblicana*, Milan: Giuffrè.

Petrocelli, C. (1994) 'Cornelia, la Matrona' in A. Fraschetti (ed.) *Roma al Femminile*, pp. 21–70, Bari: Laterza.

Phillips, J.E. (1978) 'Roman Mothers and the Lives of their Adult Daughters', *Helios*, 6: 69–80.

Rawson, B. (ed.) (1991) *Marriage, Divorce and Children in Ancient Rome*, Oxford: Oxford University Press.

Rawson, E. (1976) 'The Ciceronian Aristocracy and its Properties', in M.I. Finley (ed.) *Studies in Roman Property*, pp. 85–102, Cambridge: Cambridge University Press.

Richardson, L. (1992) *A New Topographical Dictionary of Ancient Rome*, Baltimore, MD: Johns Hopkins University Press.

Scullard, H.H. (1951) *Roman Politics 220–150*, Oxford: Clarendon.

—— (1970) *Scipio Africanus: Soldier and Politician*, London: Thames and Hudson.

Sherwin-White, A.N. (1966) *The Letters of Pliny. A Historical and Social Commentary*, Oxford: Clarendon.

Steedman, C. (1989) 'Women's Biography and Autobiography: Forms of History, Histories of Form', in H. Carr (ed.) *From My Guy to Sci Fi*, pp. 98–111, Pandora: London.

Stegman, H. (1997) 'Cornelia', *Neue Pauly. Enzyklopädie der Antike*, Band 3: col. 166, Stuttgart: Metzler.

Stockton, D. (1979) *The Gracchi*, Oxford: Clarendon.

Trevelyan, R. (1976) *The Shadow of Vesuvius*, London: Michael Joseph/Folio Society.

Walbank, F.W. (1979) *A Historical Commentary on Polybius*, vol. 3, Oxford: Clarendon.

Wood, S.E. (1999) *Imperial Women. A Study in Public Images, 40 BC–AD 68*, Leiden: Brill (*Mnemosyne* Supplement 194).

Woodcock, I. (1999) 'Inventing the "First Lady" Role: The Empress Livia and the Public Sphere', unpublished doctoral thesis, University of Queensland, Brisbane, Australia.

Zevi, F. (ed.) (2003) *John H. D'Arms: Romans on the Bay of Naples and Other Essays on Roman Campania*, Bari: Edipuglia.

Zanker, P. (1988) *The Power of Images in the Age of Augustus*. Reprinted from the German original, trans. H.A. Shapiro. Ann Arbor: University of Michigan Press.

Annotated index of ancient authors (*conspectus auctorum*)

Abbreviations

I know how difficult it is for non-classical readers to penetrate the 'codes' used by ancient historians for ancient authors and their works. For the convenience of the reader, I have included in the alphabetical list below the abbreviations I use throughout, together with authors' approximate bio-dates (where known).

The standard abbreviations are listed at the beginning of classical dictionaries. The works of Gaius Gracchus, Fannius and other second century BCE orators/authors survive only in fragmentary form (chiefly reconstructed from quotes and references to them in better preserved writings). These can be found in:

ORF, H. Malcovati (ed.) (1953) *Oratorum Romanorum Fragmenta Liberae Rei Publicae,* (Fragments of Roman Republican Orators) 4th ed. reproduced photographically 1975 from H. Malcovati (ed.), 2nd ed., 1953, Turin: Paravia, fr. 47, **69n.32, 71n.53**; 61, **69n.25**; 65–66, **69n.26**; 197 ff., **29, 70n.44**.

Many Stoic works have also been collected from scattered sources:

SVF, Stoicorum Veterum Fragmenta (Stoic Fragments), vol. III., pp. 210–213, **74n.38**.

Inscriptions are found in collections such as:

CIL, Corpus Inscriptionum Latinarum (Corpus of Latin Inscriptions) (Mommsen *et al.* Berlin, 1862 –)

AELIAN, Claudius Aelianus, *c.* 165–235 CE, born Praeneste (Palestrina), Italy: *HV (Historia Varia* = Diverse Histories/Historical Miscellany) 14.45, **77n.4**.

AMMIANUS MARCELLINUS, *c.* 330–395 CE, born Syrian Antioch: XIIII.6.11 = Zonar.ix.3, **66n.15**.

APPIAN, Appianos, *c.* late first century – 160+ CE, from Alexandria (Egypt). Appian's account of Roman wars is arranged by region and the nationality of the enemy: BC (*Bella civilia* = The Civil Wars) 1.1–26, **68n.9, 70n.42**; 1.9–11, **69n.17**; 1.12, **71n.46**; 1.19–20, **17**; 1.20, **13**; *Hisp. (Hispanica* = The Spanish Wars) 38, **73n.27**.

AUCTOR (anonymous 'author'): *Vir. Illust. (de Viris Illustribus)* 47.1, **74n.31**; 56.16, **50–1**; 57.4, **6**.

AUGUSTUS, 63 BCE–14 CE, born Gaius Octavius, later took the title 'Augustus': *RG (Res GestaeDivi Augusti* = Achievements of the Divine Augustus) 1 and *passim,* **76n.20**; 27, **58**.

AULUS GELLIUS, see GELLIUS

72nn.7,14; 34.5, 73n.21; 34.8,
73n.21; 34.52, 73n.27; 38.50 ff.,
72n.6; 38.50–57 passim, 65n.5;
38.51.1, 72n.10; 38.52.1, 45, 72n.3;
38.57, 66n.6; 38.57.3–8, 65n.4;
38.57.6, 4;38.57.8, 5; 45.8.6–7,
74n.31; *per.* (*Periochae* =
Summaries) 46, 73n.17; 46.1,
72n.12.
LUCILIUS, ca. 180–102/1 BCE, satirist,
17, 34, 47.

MACROBIUS, Macrobius Ambrosius
Theodosius, fifth century CE: *Sat.*
(*Saturnalia*) 3.164, 75n.47.
MARCUS AURELIUS ANTONINUS,
121–180 CE, emperor 161–180 CE:
To himself (or *Meditations*) 74n.33.
MARTIAL, Marcus Valerius Martialis,
c. 40–100 CE, born Bilbao (Bilbilis),
Spain: *Epigrammata* (Epigrams),
11.104:1,17–20, 49.
MUSONIUS RUFUS, Gaius, first
century CE, Roman Stoic
philosopher, 74n.33.

OROSIUS, fifth century CE: *Histories
against the Pagans* 5.12.9, 74n.41.

PLINY the Elder (Plin.), Gaius Plinius
Secundus, 23–79 CE, from Comum
(Como) N. Italy: *NH/HN* (*Historia
Naturalis* = Natural History) 7.57,
7, 12, 67n.30; 7.122, 6, 74n.30,
75n.2; 33.14.1, 72n.11; 34.31 (14),
56; 34.36, 73n.17; 35.114,139,
76n.14.
PLINY the Younger (Plin.), Gaius
Plinius Caecilius Secundus, *c.* 61–113
CE, nephew of Pliny the Elder, from
Comum (Como), N. Italy: *Ep.*
(*Epistulae* = Letters) 2.17.8, 75n.48;
3.16, 67n.32, 5.16, 76n.10; 6.16,20,
75n.46; 7.19, 67n.32.
PLUTARCH (Plut.), *c.* 45–125 CE,
born Coronea in Boeotia (Greece).
Author of *Parallel Lives* of Greeks
and Romans, usually separated into
individual *Lives* in modern editions:
Aem.P. (*Life* of Aemilius Paulus)
6.5, 75n.49; 18.35.5, 40; 28.6,
75n.49; 32–34, 73n.29; 34, 73n.20;
35, 68n.5; 35.1, 73n.20; 39.5,
72n.12, 73n.22; 39.8–10, 73n.17;

Apophth. Lak. (= Sayings of Spartan
Women) 9, 66n.10; *Life of Aristides*
1,1, 66n.16; *Cat.mai.* (*Life* of Cato
the Elder) 2.4, 72n.5; 2.5, 74n.31; 3,
72n.6; 3.5, 65n.5; 4.4–6, 73n.23;
4.5–6, 36; 4.6, 38; 11, 72n.7; 14.2,
8, 36; 15, 72n.6; 15.3, 70n.30; 18.2,
65n.5; 19.5, 73n.23; 22.(1–5), 40;
22.7, 74n.31; *Con. Praec*
(*Coniugalia Praecepta* = Marital
Precepts, from his *Moralia*) 145 E,
75n.3; *Cor.* (*Coriolanus*) 33–6, 11;
GG (*Life* of Gaius Gracchus) 2,
69n.28; 2–8, 23; 4, xiii, 21, 29, 30,
31; 4–18, 68n.9; 4.3, 28; 4.3–4, 29,
30; 4.4, 11; 5, 29; 13.2, 22, 69n.27,
70n.43; 15, 25; 15.2, 71n.53; 18,
30; 18.3, 29; 19, 11, 25, 48, 69n.27,
70n.44; 19.1, 29, 74n.41; 19.2, 44;
19.3–4, 56; 19.4, 74n.37; *M. Ant.*
(*Marcus Antonius* = Mark Anthony)
53, 76n.18; *Life of Marius*, 71n.51;
Moralia 241D, 66n.10; *Phocion*
19.3, 66n.10; *TG* (*Life* of Tiberius
Gracchus) 1.3, 4, 75n.4; 1.4–5, 6;
1.4–6, 75n.2; 1.6, 51; 1.7, 7; 4.1–4,
66n.7; 4.3, 16, 66n.8; 4.5, 12; 5–6,
16, 68n.14; 8–20, 68n.9; 8.5, 20;
8.6, 42, 61, 69n.13, 75n.43; 8.7,
xiii, 18, 31, 70n.44; 9, 20; 9–10,
69n.17; 10.1, 71n.46; 17.5–6,
69n.13; 20.4–7, 75n.44; 21.7,
68n.7.
POLYBIUS (Polyb.), c. 204–122 BCE,
Greek from Megalopolis: *Histories*
3.91.3–4, 47; 6.16, 65n.2; 6.53, (1),
(2), (6–8), 40; 11.33.7, 73n.27;
18.35, 72n.12; 26.21.1.9, 68n.5;
28.1–6, 40; 29.20.1–4, 74n.31;
31.6–8, 16; 31.22.1–4, 73n.17;
31.23–30, 66n.20, 72n.11, 73n.18;
31.25–7, 68n.5; 31.25–30, 37;
31.25 (24.) 5–6, 33; 31.25.9,
73n.18; 31.26, 27, 66n.9;
31.26.1–10, 71n.48; 31.26.3–4,
34; 31.26 (xxxii.12).6–7, 38;
31.26.10, 73n.21; 31.27.1–16,
66n.14; 31.28.3, 73n.22; 31.28.7–9,
73n.21; 31.30, 73n.18.1–4; 31.49,
73n.27.

QUINTILIAN (Quint.), Marcus Fabius
Quintilianus, *c.* 35 – 90+ CE, born
Calagurris (Calahorra), Spain : *Inst.*

Or. (*Institutions of oratory*) 1.1.6,
28, 53.

SALLUST, Gaius Sallustius Crispus, *c.*
86–35 BCE, born Amiternum,
Central Italy: *BJ* (*Bellum
Jugurthinum* = War with Jugurtha)
71n.51.
SCIPIO AEMILIANUS, fr. (Fragments)
20, 75n.45.
Scriptores Historiae Augustae, (*SHA*),
Authors of the Imperial History –
see Historia Augusta.
SENECA the Elder (Sen.), Marcus
Annaeus Seneca, *c.* 55 BCE–40 CE,
born Corduba (Cordoba), Spain:
Quaest. nat. (*Quaestiones naturales*
= Natural Investigations) 1.17.8,
66n.15.
SENECA the Younger (Sen.), Lucius
Annaeus Seneca, *c.* 4 BCE–65 CE,
born Cordoba (Cordoba), Spain: *On
the Constancy of the Wise Man*
12.3, 43, 74n.38; *Ep.Mor.*
(*Epistulae Morales* = Moral Epistles)
74n.33; 9.9.1, 76n.10; 86.4, 45; *ad
Helviam* (consolatory letter to his
mother) 12.6, 66n.15; 14.3.3,
69n.16; 16.5–6, 25; 16.6, 7, 21,
69n.23, 76n.1; 17.1–3, 76n.10;
17.3, 55; 17.3–5, 43, 76n.1; *ad
Marciam* (letter of condolence)
1.1–5, 67n.31; 2.3–5, 55; 16.3, 25,
54; 16.6, 76n.1.
SUETONIUS (Suet.), Gaius Suetonius
Tranquillus, *c.* 69–140 CE, author of
Lives of the Emperors/Caesars, listed
under the names of individual

emperors: *Aug.* (*Divi Augusti Vita* =
Life of the Divine Augustus) 34,
76n.17; *Nero,* (*Life* of Nero) 6,
77n.2; 52, 74n.34.
SVF (Stoic Fragments) III. pp. 210–213,
74n.38.

TACITUS (T. or Tac.), Cornelius
Tacitus, *c.* 56–118 CE, born Vasio,
near the Rhône: *Agric.* (*Agricola*,
biography of his father-in-law) 1.1,
xi; 4.4, 74n.34; *Ann.*(*Annales* or
Histories) 4.34–5, 67n.31; 4.53.3,
77n.2; 15.63, 76n.2; *Dialogus* 28,
53, 75n.28.

VALERIUS MAXIMUS (Val.Max.),
early first century CE (*fl.* during rule
of emperor Tiberius 14–27 CE):
Facta et dicta memorabilia
(Memorable Deeds and Sayings) 2.8,
73n.26; 2.10.2, 74n.42; 3.8.6, 12,
31; 4.2.3, 65n.4; 4.4 pr, 44, 66n.10;
4.4, xii, xv, 66n.16; 4.4.9, 73n.17;
4.4.10, 66n.15; 4.6.1, 6, 50; 4.7.1,
74n.43; 5.10.2, 68n.5; 6.7.1, 50;
9.7.2, 25, 71n.53.
VARRO, Marcus Tertius Varro,
116–27 BCE, born Reate, Italy: *RR*
(*De re rustica*) 3.16.2, 73n.17.
VEL(L)EIUS PATERCULUS, Gaius
(Vel.Pat.), *c.* 19 BCE–30 CE, born
Campania, S. Italy: 2.2, 19; 2.2.3,
69n.17.
VITRUVIUS, first century BCE: *Arch.*
(*de Architectura* = On Architecture)
1.2.7; 6.4.1, 75n.48.

Index

Note the following:

- all dates are BCE unless otherwise specified and appear in brackets, as (146) etc.
- Roman men's forenames (*praenomina*) had standard abbreviations: C= Gaius, Cn. = Gnaeus, L. = Lucius, M.= Marcus, P. = Publius, Q. = Quintus, T. = Titus, Ti. = Tiberius.
- A Roman noble family is referred to collectively by the plural form of both family names, e.g. Cornelii Scipiones (singular Cornelius Scipio), or only by the last name – Scipiones.
- Well-known figures appear under the obvious letter, eg 'G' for 'Gracchi', 'C' for Cicero, but otherwise under family (gentile) name, e.g. Mucii Scaevolae. Thus the index entry for Lucius Aemilius Paulus appears as: Aemilius Paulus, L.
- *passim* means 'throughout, in different places', e.g. Chapter 3 *passim* (throughout Chapter three)
- some entries without page references (e.g. Hera, individual Caecilii Metelli) are included for background information.
- m. = married
- b. = born
- cos. = consul

Julia Augusti

Elaine Fantham

Julia, the only daughter of Emperor Augustus, became a living example of the Augustan policy. By her marriage and motherhood she encapsulated the Augustan reforms of Rome and helped secure a dynasty.

An unidentified scandal, distorted or concealed in the ancient sources which led to her summary banishment, has discredited Julia, or at least clothed her in mystery. However, studying the abundant historical evidence available, this biography illustrates each stage of Julia's life in remarkable detail:

- her childhood – taken from her divorced mother to become part of a complex and unstable family structure
- her youth – set against the brilliant social and cultural life of the new Augustan Rome
- her marriages – as tools for Augustus' plans for succession
- Julia's defiance or her father's publicized moral regime, and implicit exposure of his hypocrisy by claiming the same sexual liberty he had once enjoyed

Reflecting new attitudes, and casting fresh light on their social reality, this accessible but penetrating portrait from one of the foremost scholars of Augustan literature and history will delight, entertain and inform anyone interested in this engaging Classical figure.

ISBN10: 0–415–33145–5 (hbk)
ISBN10: 0–415–33146–3 (pbk)

ISBN13: 978–0–415–33145–6 (hbk)
ISBN13: 978–0–415–33146–3 (pbk)

Medea

Emma Griffiths

Medea, the sorceress of Greek myth and Euripides' vengeful heroine, is famed for the murder of her children after she is banished from her own family and displaced by a new wife. Her reputation as a wronged 'everywoman' of Greek tragedy has helped engender her lasting appeal to the modern age. However, this firmly rooted status has also caused many of the intricacies of her timeless tale to be overlooked.

Emma Griffiths brings into focus previously unexplored themes of the Medea myth, along with providing an incisive introduction to the story and its history. Viewed within its context, the tale reveals fascinating insights into ancient Greece and its ideology, the importance of children, the role of women, and the position of the outsider and barbarian.

The critically sophisticated analysis, expressed in clear and accessible terms, proceeds to examine the persistence of the Medea myth through ancient Rome to the modern day. Placing the myth within a modern context and into analytical frameworks such as psychoanalysis, Griffiths highlights Medea's position in current classical study, as well as her lasting appeal. A vivid portrait of a woman empowered by her exclusion from society, alive with passion and the suffering of wounded love, this book is an indispensable guide to a fascinating mythical figure.

ISBN10: 0–415–30069–X (hbk)
ISBN10: 0–415–30070–3 (hbk)

ISBN13: 978–0–415–30069–X (hbk)
ISBN13: 978–0–415–30070–3 (pbk)